I Can Hear The Applause

Adult Language...Some Nudity

Lisa Medford
with
Jeanne Gulbranson

All names, dates, places and events are presented from the
archives of Lisa Medford's memories

All photographs in *I Can Hear the Applause* are from Lisa
Medford's personal collection

Front and Back Cover Photos: Lisa Medford in Femme de
Paris, 1968

Published by Emperor Penguin

Edited by Jessica Loving

ISBN: 1453834427
ISBN-13: 9781453834428

Books by Jeanne Gulbranson

Pink Leadership:
15 Life Lessons for Women Leaders

Be the Horse or the Jockey:
110 Tips and Techniques for Followers...and Leaders

Table of Contents

Lisa's Acknowledgements

There are special people who made (and still make) significant contributions to my life. Although you'll meet many of them in this book, there are several others who deserve their own applause. Please put your hands together for my "backstage" crew.

Mom and Dad, Alice and Icer Malouf, who taught me to be independent and a self-starter, and to my Grandma Sadie for making me tough enough to live through being an independent self-starter.

My four sisters, Barbara Joseph-Hill, Karen Callan, Joanna Staudinger, and Janis Hart, who along with Gerri Nelson, the "sixth Malouf sister," completed my enduring family—that family that has always been there for me during the good and the not-nearly-as-spectacular times.

My dear friends, Jeanie Stevenson and Mary O'Keefe, who kept hounding me to get off my butt and finish this book.

My smart, funny special friends whose delightful memories of fun times and lots of laughter also could have been included in this book. But, can you imagine a 1,000 page book? Those friends are Jackie (Gypsy Flash) Flink, Sunny Tomblin, Norton Styne, Tony Cimber, Annie Planche, and Henric Larsen. Thanks for the memories!

My "medical team," for keeping me alive and kicking and smiling, smiling, smiling through life. They are my physician, Dr. Evan Allen, my chiropractor, Dr. Jason Insera, and my dentist, Dr. Kevin Moore. It's amazing what those three can do with the miracles of modern medicine!

And to my co-author Jeanne's husband, Bill Gulbranson, who enthusiastically and patiently "gave good audience" hour after hour while I told my stories and Jeanne wrote and wrote and wrote.

I hope that you can all hear the applause!

Introduction

I've never wanted to disappoint my audience, so let's make sure we're on the same page from the get-go. If you think you bought a history book of Las Vegas, or Hollywood or the Russian Invasion of Czechoslovakia, then you should probably wrap this up for a Christmas present. This isn't a book full of dates and times to memorize. Hell, I'm not even so sure about some of the dates myself; I've been around for awhile now! So, not to worry, there won't be a quiz when you're finished reading.

This is **my** history in Vegas, and Hollywood and Prague. It's the way I lived and the way I remember all those way-too-interesting times and places. And mostly, it's the people I crashed into on my journey through 70+ years. Most of the times were out-of-control fun, and the people were stand-up fabulous; although I also came across a few flat tires in my journey. But added together, they all have made one helluva life!

People who are more "settled" (and probably more stable) than I am have told me repeatedly, "You should make your Plan A and follow it while having a Plan B, just in case." Screw that. I never had a Plan A. I just went right to Plan B. Travel along the road, come to a crossroads, and pick the direction that feels good at the time. It may not be the "right" direction, but if it felt good at the start, it might feel good at the end.

When I was 18, I went on Mr. Toad's Wild Ride at the just-opened Disneyland in Anaheim. Mr. Toad, you had nothing on me. You should have been along for my wild ride! Your little green butt would have been sitting on my lap in the back of a big, black stretch limo with Cher, Cary Grant, or Steve McQueen, or maybe Elton John and Ringo Starr, or a collection of other fabulous celebrities. Mr. Toad, you and I would have ridden with some really great people and a few of those flat tires I told you I came across. A short 50 years later, you'd have joined me in the front seat when I was the celebrities-choice limo driver in Vegas. It all worked for me. I was still in the limo—still on Lisa's Wild Ride!

So, if you're reading this book for its "historical value"... sorry for you. But if you want to join me on Lisa Malouf Medford's Wild Ride...keep reading and hang on!

Tropicana, 1961

ONE

The First Nude in Vegas

"Hey, kid, do **you** have any tits?"

"What? Of course, I do."

"Okay, let's see 'em. Maybe you can be our nude showgirl."

That's not how this conversation is supposed to go. I'm a 19-year-old, ready-to-take-on-the-world, newly married little darling of Hollywood. I'm also a convent-educated, good Catholic girl who still tries on bathing suits in a closet so my sisters won't see too much skin. Modesty is next to godliness and all that. I'm supposed to show my tits to these two cigar-chomping guys who are stuffed into my dog-house-sized office at 2:30 in the morning? Oh, what the hell. It's late. I'm tired. I'll show 'em. I pull up my crisply ironed white blouse, lift my bra, and say, "There ya go...tits."

Sammy Lewis leans forward, takes a good look, and says, "Yeah, they're fine. You're the showgirl. Now let's find another one that matches you."

And that was where I started my journey to becoming the first nude showgirl in Vegas and a part of my city's exciting history—a crappy little office in Andy Anderson's modeling agency in Hollywood in the middle of the night in January 1957.

I married Mike Mancuso not long after graduating from Immaculate Heart High School in Los Angeles. My parents made it perfectly clear that I couldn't move out of the house until I was married, and living at home was definitely going to cramp my freewheeling lifestyle. I wanted to move out, so I got married. Simple fix. Then, my parents did what parents do. My mother threw an elaborate second wedding for 200 of her "closest friends" to attend six months after our runaway wedding in Vegas, and my father gave Mike a job.

Life was good. I had a sexy-looking Sicilian husband who made decent money (thanks, Dad), and I was going to college (thanks, Dad) and working as a freelance and agency model. (I had only been model material for about a year though. I must have done something as a baby to really piss off God. I blossomed from the Prettiest Baby in L.A. in 1939, to 5'8" and scary-skinny, with a nose you could use for an umbrella, by the age of 13. I was so ugly that when my mother's friends first saw me, they used to say, "Oh dear. Well, I'm sure she's a sweet girl." I spent the year after high school drinking protein and egg shakes and eating Bob's Big Boy fries smothered in chocolate ice cream. And I got a nose job. By the time I was 18, my body caught up with my height and there I was modeling on runways and posing for top photographers. (Thanks for that second chance, God.)

It was early in my first modeling year that I became Lisa Britton. The 1939 Prettiest Baby was actually born Loretta Malouf. What kind of name was that for a future star? Loretta Malouf sounded like a good Catholic girl who worked at Kresge's five and dime. I needed something that would sparkle on a marquee and pop out at you in Variety magazine. One day, just before an upcoming photo shoot for Warner Brothers, about 12 models were hanging out in Andy Anderson's offices.

Loretta Malouf, age 13. See the nose?

We all decided that it was time to "go Hollywood" and pick our stage names. The right names in the '50s were short and simple, probably because neon lights weren't cheap. We thought up a dozen generic first names and put them in a bowl. I picked first... Loretta became Lisa. We tossed around last names that seemed to go with Lisa and decided that Britton was the one. Faster than a Vegas wedding—Loretta Malouf became Lisa Britton! *Try it. Say "Lisa Britton." Feels pretty good in your mouth, doesn't it?*

I had found Andy Anderson in a trade magazine ad, and it was one of those "come to the crossroads and take the path that looks right at the time" decisions. Andy looked like Gabby Hayes, only scruffier and a lot smellier. He had gnarly toes that poked out of his Jesus shoes. His "business attire" was completed by a not-real-clean plaid shirt. He looked eccentric and arty to me. (*Hey, I was a kid! Besides, the big photographers went to him, and they all looked gnarly too.*)

Between my own contacts and Andy's agency, I was having a good run and a great time doing pinup work, runway gigs, and trade shows, and posing for magazine and record album covers. I was on too-many-to-count covers of Man's Magazine. (I was always in danger of getting eaten by snakes or drowning or going over a cliff while being rescued by some hunk.) I paraded around at trade shows looking incredibly charmed by my clients' welding machines or boats, and I posed for a series of ads for a knitting machine. (Looking at those ads today, it's pretty obvious from the look on my face that I had no idea what to do with a knitting machine.) I got to wear great clothes (and keep some of them), get pampered by makeup people and hairstylists, and have people tell me all day long just how cute I was—and they gave me money for that!

Yep, life was good. What I didn't do was show a lot of skin. This was the mid-fifties: fast cars, pony tails, hanging out at the soda fountain with your guy, and only hinting at what was under those crinoline skirts. We perfected the art of the tease in the '50s and learned how to "make 'em beg." This turned out to be an important life skill for me—I just didn't realize it at the time.

The job orders were coming in as fast and as many as I could handle, and photographers were asking specifically for "Lisa." I learned real fast that it wasn't good enough to give an employer—any employer—the minimum of what they thought they paid for. I always made sure I brought "extras" to the job. When the client or the boss is pleasantly surprised, they remember you, and the calls and raises and promotions keep coming. That something extra in my early days of modeling meant that I had to do more than just look great. For example, models didn't always show up. I don't mean "didn't show up on time;" they just didn't go to one shoot if they'd gotten a better one. Not me…I was there early every time to help the photographer set his lighting and to charm the client and the crew into good moods before our shoot. I'd bring accessories that I thought might work with the costumes, just in case we needed a little change in the look. Give 'em more and you get more—worked then, and it worked for me for the nearly 50 years to come.

Then, Andy had a heart attack and landed in the hospital. I went to visit him not only because he was always good to me, but also to figure out how I was going to get my bookings. While we talked about his heart and health and gossiped about who was doing what to whom, he said, "Kid, you're the only one who knows how to run things around there. Here's the key to the place. Run it like it's your own." Sure, I could do that. After all, I was 19, married, a model, and a college student with a kick-ass, look-out-world-I've-arrived attitude.

Now I was also running Andy's agency. (Okay, I did cream off some of the really great jobs for myself, but I made sure that all the other models were working and making good money. I was, and still am, ambitious—not selfish.)

I went right from the hospital to Andy's (now my) office to look over my new kingdom. Things were as they should be. I was in charge. Hmmm. I hadn't really noticed before just how crappy the place was. Sitting right on Santa Monica Boulevard, you'd think it would be a little classier. But, *classy* was not the word. *Goodwill-shitty* was the word. There wasn't one piece of furniture that matched, unless you counted that every piece in the place was beat up and ugly. It's a good thing the windows were so dirty because that made it hard to see the coffee stains on the brown corduroy sofa with the stuffing sticking out. I didn't even want to think about what the non-coffee stains could be. Good Catholic girls shouldn't even know about "casting couches."

We had another room besides the "corporate office," where derelicts and never-going-to-get-modeling-jobs losers hung out all day. I tried not to think about that room or the strange noises that came out of it sometimes.

Well, at least we had a few cool neighbors at our office. Harold Lloyd, the silent comedy actor and producer was right across the hall. Actually, I thought he was a nice old guy until I spent more time at Andy's. Then Harold made me crazy running in to use my phone all the time. He was so cheap that he didn't want to use his own. Okay, so it wasn't great; but now, it was mine.

Not long after taking on my new job, the producers, Sammy Lewis and Danny Dare, walked into the office looking for Andy. Nope, no Andy here…it was just me. That was good enough for them. The minute I saw them, I knew this was going to be an amazing ride. Sammy and Danny didn't look like the usual unshaved photographers who ran in and out. They were dressed to the nines—expensive suits, ties, overcoats, and hats—and they smelled like successful men were supposed to. They were producing Harry Belafonte's show at the Riviera and wanted to get the jump on what would become a significant part of the Vegas image—nude extravaganzas on the Strip. Harold Minsky was planning to bring in Minsky's Follies to take advantage of a newly passed Vegas ordinance that would allow complete nudity. (Well, almost completely nude. The politicians' working definition of *nude* seemed to mean "still covering up a few square inches.") But Sammy and Danny wanted to be the ground breakers for "taking it off" in Vegas before Minsky's girls showed up.

The way Sammy explained the nude part was like this: "Still have to cover up the nipples, like the sight of a couple of pink eyes is going to kill somebody. And we need to figure out how to get a small patch over the prime 'real estate.'" (From the beginnings of Vegas up to today, Sin City has always been about the fantasy—it's all "smoke and mirrors." Even "nude" was...almost nude.)

The tops were definitely coming off, and Sammy and Danny wanted to unveil the treasures first. But there was another strange clause in that first Vegas nudity law. The nude show-girl couldn't move while she was on stage. She had to stand still for her whole number. High on looks and low on talent—if you had the body and could stay upright for 10 minutes, you could do the job! (Almost immediately after that breast-baring, Vegas history-making, the Las Vegas City Council got a lot happier with bare nipples and nude showgirls, so they decided that moving around nude wasn't a criminal act. They saw standing-room-only crowds and did the math for all the city revenue. Who said our politicians weren't visionaries?)

Vegas has made a fortune from skin. You may read that Harold Minsky brought the first topless show to Vegas. No, he didn't. Sammy Lewis and Danny Dare did it—a good three months before Minsky's uncovered beauties showed up.

Sammy and Danny placed their order for two girls that looked exactly alike. The girls would flank the stage, one standing far right and the other far left, with the "moving-around" showgirls and dancers between them. The nudes were going to hold perfectly still under a fountain, looking like ancient Italian statues, only without the arms cut off. What a great gig! A 30-day run in a Harry Belafonte show, paying $250 week—didn't get too much sweeter than that in 1957! I jumped right on it, calling all the great-looking girls I knew, placing ads in the *LA Times*, the *Hollywood Reporter*, the *New York Times*, papers in Chicago, Denver, Dallas—anywhere I thought there might be two wanna-be nudes. I interviewed what seemed like 200 women. Some were too old, too young, too fat, too skinny, too ugly….all too something. And the pictures were coming in! Craziness! I was getting naked pictures from 70-year-old women and mothers sending pictures of their 12-year-old daughters. The first group was just nasty looking, and the mothers pimping their daughters for a nudie show—that was just really wrong! And although I found some great looking girls who were at least close to legal age, but not so far beyond it that they were collecting Social Security, I couldn't put two together that looked alike. (There was one that was perfect—a tall, blonde, busty girl who looked just like Anita Ekberg. But I couldn't find her twin, and I didn't think Anita would be interested.)

About a month after their first visit, Sammy and Danny showed up again at 7:00 p.m. at my hole-in-the wall office, puffing on their cigars…and just puffing in general.

"Sweetheart, where's our girls?" Sammy puffed. "We open in three days. We need those nudes! It's just three days away!"

"I've got one, but I can't match her up," I said.

I showed them the Ekberg look-alike, and we poured through hundreds of photos (again!) looking for her match. No luck. Then we went through all of the photos again, looking for any other two that matched. This was nuts! How hard is it to find two gorgeous girls that look alike? Harder than we thought. If she had great legs, she had no tits. Great tits, no ass. Great legs, tits, and ass…she had a cow-face. We found a 6' blonde who had it all, and a 5'4" brunette. We kept looking, the clock kept ticking, and my husband wouldn't stop calling to see when I was coming home. There was so much cigar smoke in that doghouse office, I figured I'd just eat it for dinner.

Too soon it was 2:30 a.m., and Sammy asked the question that started my Vegas showgirl ride: "Hey, sweetheart, do you have any tits?" We went back to the ruffled up pile of pictures to find one that matched me. There it was—a Brazilian beauty who used the name Jeannette Russell professionally. I called her in the middle of the night and told her to pack. I called home and told my husband, "We're going to Vegas, baby!" Then I called one of our out-of-work models and told her she was taking over "my" office for a month. Everything was taken care of, and it wasn't even 3:00 in the morning yet. Damn, I was good.

As I started to pack, I wondered how long it would take me to get over that "don't let strangers see the jewels" hang-up I had. Okay, probably not too long. For $250 week, I could get over just about anything. Besides, I was really comfortable going to Vegas to work since I'd practically grown up there. I'd go along with my parents when my dad used to play poker with Benjamin "Bugsy" Siegel and the rest of the boys. "Uncle Ben" used to braid my hair for me. I remember crying and yelling at him, "Uncle Ben, you've ruined my life," when he made one braid fat and one skinny. When I was 12 years old and saw a showgirl for the first time, with all the feathers and jewels, I declared that I'd be a showgirl when I grew up. Dad and the boys laughed—they thought that little Loretta was "so cute." They had no idea how cute I'd be as a showgirl seven years later! (I have vivid and exciting memories of being at the craps table with my parents when I was 15 and 16. Nobody asked how old I was. It was a real advantage to me then to be 5'8" and dark-haired, with a big Lebanese nose. When I finally had that nose fixed when I was 18, I looked a lot younger and my days at the craps table were over until I became a showgirl. Then nobody cared how old I was.)

I was ready to take off for Vegas by 10:00 a.m.—less than eight hours after my middle-of-the-night proof to Sammy and Danny that I did have tits—but husband Mike wasn't too keen about tagging along. (Really a sweet guy, but he was a little short on adventure-seeking genes.)

"I can't just leave L.A. for Vegas. I'm working for your dad!" Mike protested. "Besides, do **you** want to tell your mom and dad that you're going to be standing on stage naked?"

"Not naked, Mike—nude. Naked is gross. Nude is art," was my sophisticated response. (At 19, I thought I was the most worldly woman in L.A. It took me 10 more years to figure out that I didn't know shit.)

"We'll tell them that I have a 30-day tour modeling really high-end clothes all over the country and you have to go with me. Dad will hold the job for you. What's he going to do? Let us live with them when we come back?"

But poor short-sighted Mike just couldn't make the leap and join me on the adventure. He stayed home and did whatever boring thing he usually did. (Looking back, that was the beginning of the end for Mike and me. "Get onboard and hang on, Mike…or I'm riding solo!")

I threw together my clothes, picked up Jeannette, stuffed my parakeet, Elvis, and my French Poodle, Joey, into my 1957 red and white Thunderbird, and the four of us headed down Highway 91 to Vegas. On the way out of town, we stopped and I picked up a bunch of could-be-from-anywhere postcards and addressed them to my parents, using different pens. I had a plan to shore up the lie to my parents. While we were in Vegas, I'd meet people from Chicago, Dallas, New York— from all over. I'd quickly fill out a postcard that read, "Things are going great in (name of the tourists' city)" and ask them to mail it for me when they returned home. The celebrity-struck tourists would mail the cards, my parents would believe the fashion modeling story, and everything would be good.

Until the night my first cousin sat in the front row of my show. Then, things were not so good.

Driving from L.A. to Vegas in the '50s was a nightmare, although we didn't recognize how really bad it was then. There was only one way to get there, so we just held on and roared down the 91—we were goin' to Vegas! Trust me when I tell you, it was not a great drive. The road was so bumpy that you got a butt massage the whole way. That would have felt good for 30 minutes, but for almost five hours...torture! Besides getting a pancake ass, you had to try to outrun the dust devils dumping sand in your open car windows and swerve to miss the big snakes curled up on the road. It was like going through the Reptile House at the zoo, only without the cages and the cotton candy. The two-lane road was full of other snakes, too. Drunks heading into Vegas or coming out meant you really had to drive the whole way there instead of just holding on to the wheel and zoning out. (Some things don't change. The highway in and out of Vegas is still full of drunks, although the road's a little wider and there are fewer actual reptiles.) There weren't a lot of places to eat along the way back then, unless you weren't too particular. If you just didn't care, you could always eat the road kill that was frying on the blacktop in the 100+ degree heat. Still, the pain of the trip barely registered in the anticipation of the new adventure.

You'd think that Jeannette and I would have been over-the-top excited and talking all the way about our great showgirl job. Nope. We were mostly concerned about dodging snakes and, "Where are we going to get a great cheeseburger?" What did we know? We were 19 years old, and we thought we'd already seen and done just about everything that counted. We were in for some real surprises! We did notice that all the other drivers (at least the sober ones) were grinning at us when they came close. We'd smile back, figuring they were admiring the two cute girls or the bird and the dog in the back seat. Maybe they were, or maybe they were grinning about the sticker I'd put in the porthole of my Thunderbird that read, "Made in Hollywood by Just About Everybody."

We sure didn't waste any time wondering if we could do the job as we roared into Vegas. How hard could it be to stand still for 10 minutes, with your arms in the air, looking gorgeous? (It was like one of those flag-holder jobs on the road construction crews, except that we'd look a whole lot better. You see the cracks of their butts, too...but ours were cuter.) I knew I had the body for the job. I was 38-25-35 (without silicone yet), and I had a bag full of makeup and strong arms. Lots of people told me that I had a Sophia Loren look. At 19, I thought that she might have a Lisa Britton look.

The only show-related talk during the drive was figuring out how much money a minute we were going to make. Let's see: two shows a night, seven nights a week, being on stage for 10 minutes each show, and getting paid $250 a week. That's more than $1.75 a minute! (*I can wait for you here while you check my math.*) We'd have plenty of time to lie around the pool and go shopping, and we'd have the money to do it with. Sweet.

When we got to Vegas, Jeannette and I dumped our stuff in a shit-hole motel for the first night and ran out to meet Lloyd Lambert, the costume designer. We were really excited to see what incredible stuff he was creating for us. We already knew about Lambert, who was the Bob Mackie of his day. His specialty was headdresses, and we just knew we'd be buried in feathers, furs, and rhinestones. We were ready—bring on the glamour!

When we saw the costumes at Lambert's office, 30 minutes into our Vegas adventure, we were not so ready. Lambert handed us each a set of pasties—pointy, silver, swirly, metal, stripper-ugly pasties that were supposed to fit (painfully) over our nipples.

I told him, "These are vulgar! We shouldn't wear these pointy things!"

Lambert glared at me and replied, "Hey, you're going to be standing there naked, and you're worried about being vulgar?"

"Not naked...nude. Nude is classy," I replied. Damn, just like my husband Mike! I thought Lambert would have known the difference. Okay, Lloyd, let me show you how it's done. It was time to start bringing out the "little extra" for this job.

I saw some silver glitter sitting on a shelf behind Lambert's head, reached across him to get it, and pulled some eyelash glue out of my purse. I poured a pile of glitter on his desk, took off my blouse and bra, brushed the glue all over my nipples, and poked them into the glitter. That took care of the nipple issue. (*See how quickly I got over my aversion to showing skin to strangers, or anybody? Twelve hours after lifting up my bra in Andy's office and inwardly saying, "Forgive me Father, for I have sinned," I was rubbing my bare nipples across Lloyd Lambert's desk. I was always a quick learner.*)

Now, what about the rest of it? How about the patch for the prime real estate? Lambert handed us French bikini underpants that were cheesy, flesh-colored diaper-y things with sequins all over them. Ugly, UGLY, **UGLY**!

Lambert glared again when I said, "Those don't look like 'nude' costumes. They look like baggy underpants!" I took

Lambert's scissors and cut out all the mesh and the sequins. We were left with a small patch in the front and a strip of fabric that went under our crotches and was held on with toupee tape and by scrunching up our asses. Done. We had nude costumes.

Lambert approved my creations (and subsequently got all the credit for the cool-looking outfits), and we were ready to roll...or stand still. We did the alterations on Jeannette's costume and ran over to the Riviera for our first rehearsal. Yes, we did have to practice to stand still for 10 minutes with both arms in the air. We also had to figure out where to position ourselves to hide the pipe going up our backs supplying the water for the fountains right behind us. We needed to look like the fountains—living, breathing, nude, water-spewing fountains.

It's a good thing that we saw the stage right away. I realized that when we breathed, people would be able to tell that we weren't statues. (Some asshole stagehand suggested that we don't breath for the show—obviously a minimum-wage employee.) So, I pulled out another "extra."

"Let's cover ourselves with baby oil and throw a little glitter here and there," I said. "We'll shimmer when we breathe, and it'll look like the water from the fountain is pouring over us." What's better than seeing a nude showgirl? Seeing a wet, nude showgirl!

And that made up our costumes—a handful of glitter and eyelash glue, a patch of fabric the size of a postcard with toupee tape, high heels, baby oil, and a silver hat that looked like part of the fountain.

The next two days before opening night were a non-stop blur—publicity photos, learning how to step on and off the 2' high pedestals in 3" heels without breaking an ankle, and moving out of the shit-hole motel and into the Country Club Apartments in Vegas. The apartments were stuffy little rooms, but they had swamp coolers for air-conditioning, and there was a pool. Even with all those "amenities" though, an apartment was only $50 a month. Some of the dancers from the Riviera and other hotels also stayed there, so Jeannette and I had lots of performers to hang out with. We also soon invited Belafonte's guys to move in there. Belafonte was allowed to stay in the Riviera, but not his backup guys. I'm saying "allowed" because, as you probably already know, at the time Negros couldn't stay at the Strip hotels; they had to stay out-of-sight in West Vegas. (*Don't jump on me.* Negro *was the word we used in the fifties.*) I asked the Country Club Manager if the guys could move in, and she didn't object. As long as they paid the rent, she didn't care if she filled the place with space aliens.

Belafonte's guys completed our Country Club group, and many nights you could find us at the pool, drinking and laughing about what had happened at that night's show. Sometimes, we'd all sleep around the pool just to get out of the breadbox-sized rooms and avoid the just-won't-quit drone of that great "amenity"—the swamp-cooler. I was living large—paying $50 a month rent to hang with friends, and making $250 a week. I'm telling you...it just didn't get much better than that.

We also got to meet Harry Belafonte in those first few days. We were never on stage at the same time, but we needed to know "The Man." And definitely, he was The Man! Belafonte was a total sweetheart when you got to know him, but in those first introductions, he was pretty aloof. (In later years, I wondered if it was because he was uncomfortable being the only Negro in the hotel—in any Strip hotel, actually.) He definitely stood out in a crowd. Of course, Harry was so gorgeous that you'd notice him if he was white, black, red, or lizard-skinned! Besides having "the look," you could always smell him coming, too. He wore what had to be a whole bottle of cologne every day. You sure didn't have to see him to know he was close by. Nice, expensive stuff, but…whew! Harry's manners, however, were just as perfect as his face and that great, tight body. He never came on to me or any of the other girls. He was totally devoted to his wife, and he never crossed the line with any of the showgirls. That was good and bad. Good because I wasn't there to sleep around, but bad because it spoiled me for other headliners. I thought they'd all act like Belafonte—great to have around, fun, and respectful. Not so.

When he got to know you, Harry was also a bit of a jokester. He was plagued by the desert throat that attacks all singers in Vegas and always carried around a huge glass of water. One night, he had filled his mouth with what seemed like five gallons of water. As I stepped off my pedestal at the end of my number, he spewed the water all over me. I yelped and jumped around, and both of us cracked up at the sight of all the water rolling down by baby-oiled body. Spewed on by Harry Belafonte. Yep, it's always the little things that I seem to remember and cherish.

But that first week in Vegas, opening night popped up too fast. The Riviera was loaded with excited people, backstage and out front. The word was out in the crowd that a surprise was coming up that night!

If you weren't there for that first show, I'll describe it to you. You can be there now, with me and the famous Dorothy Dorbin dancers. Go and pour a glass of something special (make sure it's a real crystal glass), and put your arm around your best girl, or lay your hand nice and easy on your best guy's thigh. No, don't grab his leg; you're not squeezing a melon. Just barely lay your hand on him. (We didn't go for public groping in the '50s. That was gross. All the girls in the '50s acted like virgins during the day and turned into "backseat Betties" at night.)

Ready to go to the show? You've got the best seats in the house because you gave the maitre d' 10 bucks. You're right up front, center stage, sitting at a table with starched white linen, real china, and crystal, and you look too fine. You both light a cigarette. The show is about to begin.

While you're getting settled into your seats, I'm backstage…and suddenly, I'm that 15-year-old beanpole with a nose again! I'm scared shitless! It's pitch black back there, and I'm pressed up against monstrous, black velvet curtains.

"Just kill me now! Smother me to death! What if they laugh? What if I fall off the pedestal? Hell, what if I can't get on the damn thing in the dark? What if they hate me? I WANT MY MOTHER!" But, wait, what's happening? I hear the call for "five minutes to show time." I get onto the pedestal, and I hear the music. The lights come on, and the curtain is going up, and I hear you, out there….clapping, and shouting, for ME!

"Okay, Mother…later." I can hear the applause.

The musicians are playing their hearts out below the stage. You don't know what the music is, but you don't care.

The curtain is coming up. From your VIP spot, you can see almost the whole small stage with just a few small turns of your head—and what a sight! The lighting is sexy silver-blue, making the stage a little dark, but not too dark to see what you've never seen in Topeka (or Cleveland or St. Paul or wherever you came from). There are dancers in perfect beat to the music, silver canoes and big fish filled with girls, a 20-foot-tall silver fountain in the center of the stage, and two showgirls in costumes like water fountains near the back of the stage.

Hey, what's that at either side of the stage? They must be nude statues, standing on those pedestals with the water coming out of their hats. About two minutes into the number, you are just leaning over to whisper, "Look at those naked fountains. They almost look alive," when you see an arm, slowly and mechanically, begin to move down. What? They're real girls! And they're naked!

The crowd is going wild—shouting and screaming, "They're real! They're alive!" The orchestra is playing louder, but you don't even notice. You're hollering too! *To be really authentic, hold your girl a little tighter, and now squeeze his thigh. You're both going to get lucky tonight. (I hope that felt good for you… it sure did for me that night!)*

That was the beginning of my 11-year romance with being a Vegas showgirl. I worked the Riviera, Dunes, Sands, Frontier, and Tropicana many times from 1957 until 1968, my last year as a show girl. I would go to Hollywood and model a little and appear on TV and in a few movies, but I'd keep driving up and down Highway 91 to be a Vegas Showgirl in the great shows like the Folies Bergere and the Casino De Paris, and in a few of the not-so-great shows. I got fired from the Frontier for beating up a security guard, but that didn't stop me from getting back on stage. I had developed "the heart of a showgirl" during that first show, and I was hooked.

I feel the need to make a small confession here—one of many confessions coming up, although some of them are a lot bigger. (I do know how to recite a list of sins. My knees still have dents because of all the time I spent kneeling in a confessional when I was a kid.) I was so naïve in 1957 that I didn't even realize what a big deal that first nude show was until 2005, the year the Riviera Hotel celebrated its 50th Anniversary. The whole nude fountain gig was just one stop in Lisa's Wild Ride back then. (*I know you think I was crazy. Hell, I was a 19-year-old '50s kid. What did I know?*)

The Riviera put my picture on a $100 chip honoring the "First Ladies of the Riviera," along with Kim Krantz and Ruth Gillis, and invited me to the gala Anniversary celebration. On the way into the party, I ran into Bob Vannucci, the President of the Riviera. I showed him that I was wearing original Riviera showgirl jewelry in honor of the occasion. (I just knew that the Riviera wanted me to have the jewels I wore, so I helped them out with their "gifting" by taking some when I left. Actually, I figured all the hotels I worked for wanted me to enjoy my show jewelry forever…so I helped out their gifting too.)

During the Anniversary party, Mr. Vannucci introduced Kim Krantz, the first dancer to sign with the Riviera, and then Ruth Gillis, the first Riviera showgirl. There was ear-crashing applause and a few appreciated catcalls.

First Ladies of the Riviera, 2005

Then he said, slowly and dramatically, "And we have Lisa Medford…the first nude showgirl in Vegas! And she's wearing the jewelry she stole from us!" As I stood up to wave to the crowd, the people were going wild—hollering and clapping and whistling. I thought, "Damn…that must have really been something!" But who knew? Did Elvis know he changed the music world the first time he swiveled his hips? Did Ray Kroc know he was changing the food world when he opened his first drive-in? Did Neil Armstrong know he was changing the whole world when he took that first step on the Moon? Well, maybe Armstrong knew. But who knew I was changing the image of Las Vegas, the greatest adult playground in the world, when I took it all off? Not me.

I was married, divorced, and then married again during the next decade, and I kept going back to Vegas. I worked for the powerful Mob bosses that owned and ran Vegas—the "boys." I respected a lot of the good ones and hated a few of the slimy bastards. I sure never worried about what to do next, though. For the next 10 years of my Wild Ride, I had a showgirl's life to turn to whenever I needed the fix of the Vegas showrooms' glamour and excitement—and whenever I needed to hear all that applause.

Lisa's Wild Ride had begun!

Classic showgirl! Tropicana in the 1960s

Two

Livin' Large in Vegas

The Heart of a Showgirl

"It's like cocaine...only a lot better. Once you feel that first rush with the lights and the music, and hear the people screaming and clapping, you're hooked. You can't just stop. Your heart would probably blow up! But, it's better than coke. They pay **you** to get the high."

As I approached my 50th birthday, that was my response to a girlfriend about why I spent 11 years, after my first nude showgirl gig, driving up and down Highway 91 to Vegas, putting on my showgirl feathers and strutting my stuff.

We both knew about cocaine highs, but I was the one who knew both kinds of rushes. And like cocaine, the need for the rush never really goes away. You can stop shoving the white stuff up your nose or quit prancing across the stage half (or all) undressed, but you never forget or stop looking for that thrill...just one more time.

I'm even older now, but believe me when I tell you, if there was a show looking for the over-70 showgirls, I'd be there— rhinestones, a G-string, and fancy jewelry and carrying around a 20-pound headdress with my 72-year-old legs. *Don't wrinkle up your nose at that. You haven't seen those hot-mama legs I've got now. Have you?*

You never stop being a showgirl. You just never stop hearing the applause. There are quite a few of us originals living in Vegas, and we get together to eat, drink, and remember those early years. Unfortunately, today there are Metamucil bottles sitting at the table where the Dom Perignon used to be. At a recent lunch, I looked at a faded, face-lifted girl reliving one of her shows and wondered, "Where did the showgirl go? I think she died and some fat, old broad took possession of her body!" Just then, my former showgirl friend turned her head just enough to play to the men at the table next to ours. That told me the showgirl was alive and well! No tits, wide ass, and stomach out to here....but heart? It's still there.

On my mostly unplanned Wild Ride, I've been an actress, a photojournalist, Cary Grant's lover, an Emmy-nominated producer, and Accounts Receivable Manager at Sony Studios. I've sold ponchos, wigs, drugs, and antiques. I've ridden in the back of the limo with the stars and in the front, driving them around. But...I'm first and forever...a showgirl.

Looking in the mirror today and asking, "Where is the showgirl today?" is a first-thing-in-the-morning wake-up call. I never minded getting old. I was actually looking forward to being old enough to do and say whatever I wanted. Old people get by with a lot of in-your-face stuff. (I mentioned that to a friend once who was horrified at that thought. "Damn, Lisa! Have you been holding back? That's real scary.") The problem is that no one ever told me getting old would hurt. It doesn't matter though. Let the orchestra begin, open the curtain, and watch me strut. I'm still kickin', just not as high.

I may not have exactly the same legs today, but I still have the heart of a showgirl.

Where does that heart come from? It comes with the flowers in your dressing room and the bosses stopping by to make sure you're happy. A friendly pat from one of the bosses lets you know you're special. (Sexual harassment? That whole concept just never registered with us. If they didn't slap you on the ass periodically, you felt neglected.)

The showgirl heart is fueled from that last look in the mirror just before you go on, when your makeup is perfect, the sparkle of the jewelry and the glittery costume is reflected in your eyes, and your tanned, lotion-soaked skin is as smooth as a bald guy's head. Like that bald head, your whole body is giving off "just stroke me" signals. You're the hottest thing walking, and you know it!

You gather with the rest of the girls to peek around the curtain as the live orchestra is tuning up. The room is filling with excited people and you can hear the clink of their crystal glasses while their cigarette smoke swirls in the air. (If you weren't there, you can't know just how sexy cigarette smoke was. Did you ever see a picture of James Dean without a cigarette? It was the sixth finger on our hand. This was the 1950s when living healthy meant...well, it didn't mean anything to us then. Why bother worrying about that stuff? We lived for today and we were immortal. Then, we drifted right into the '60s, when living healthy meant making sure that whatever we smoked or snorted or swallowed was clean. We had some different standards then.)

To a showgirl, it was a complete package. It was music playing, people laughing, crystal clinking, smoke swirling, and people waiting for you—their fantasy girl—to appear. We were the heat that was going to light their after-the-show sex, and we knew it. (Sometimes, we lit their during-the-show sex also. More than once, we'd have to tell backstage security that we had a "Loner Boner" on Table 9—some guy who just couldn't wait for the show to end.)

When you step out on that stage or descend from the ceiling on a shaky-ass, ¾" plywood platform or parade down a calf-killer staircase, the crowd goes wild. That's it—that's the highest point of the rush. You never lose the feeling that comes from knowing that every woman in the audience wants to look like you and every man wants you.

We could all hear the applause.

Between shows, you eat like a linebacker and down five or six drinks to refuel that showgirl heart. But somebody had to pay for all that feasting, and we sure didn't intend to. And we didn't need to. After the first show, you joined your admirers for dinner and drinks. Not all the admirers, though. Just the ones who could afford the Chateaubriand and strawberry crepes, the $300 bottles of wine, and the little diamond bracelets to show their appreciation for your company. I ate with the big spenders or famous people (Bear Bryant was a favorite dinner companion) or politicians (the president of Mexico, Miguel Aleman, and all his sexy-looking bodyguards placed strategically around the room) or sometimes other celebrities.

At least one time, I remember a "dinner" that went way over the top. Adnan Khashoggi, the Saudi Arabian arms dealer, took the entire showgirl line (about 10 girls) from the Sands to Paris (yes, the Paris in France) on his private jet. That shut down the show for two nights! (I never heard about what kind of arrangements were worked out, but I have to believe that Khashoggi made it worth it to the Sands.) High-rollers were the first choice for dinner companions. Entertainers and celebrities…not so much. Most of them liked the freebies as much as we did, but if they did want to leave for a quick dinner, they were apt to pick the Silver Slipper where you could get biscuits and gravy and a beer for 35 cents.

We changed out of our show costumes before dinner and into designer evening clothes. We left on all of our show makeup, including the false eyelashes. (I used to wear three pair on the top and two on the bottom. I still do when I get the showgirl feeling. It's like looking through a jungle unless you open your eyes to dinner-plate size.) We bought whatever fabulous clothes were currently showing in Vogue magazine, and we wore them every night. (Of course that was in the days when everyone, including the tourists, locals, and employees, dressed to the nines after 5:00 p.m. Wearing blue jeans and tennis shoes in a casino was unheard of! Everyone who went to or lived in Vegas then was willing to pass on, "I just want to be comfortable," for the much better feeling of, "I want to feel like I'm doing something special."

When I put on my favorite pale lavender, chiffon evening gown, with my purple fox fur, put a purple rinse through my hair so it shimmered in the candle light, and loaded on lots of sparkly jewelry, I knew I was showgirl, kick-ass gorgeous. There might be just you and him at dinner, or another showgirl might be invited, or sometimes it was the whole showgirl line. When it was the showgirl line, all heads in the restaurant would spin around! That looked like a buffet to the other diners. You knew they just wanted to lie down on your table and sample all the goodies. These between-show dinners helped your showgirl heart to keep the right rhythm until the next show. We laughed and teased and made 'em beg for it using that well-practiced life skill again. When dinner was over, we were full of great food and expensive liquor, hopefully wearing a new sparkly something, and revved up, ready to go on for one or even two more shows. Keep that showgirl heart pumping!

After the second show, the glow continues as you mix with the crowd until 2:00 in the morning and let your fans get even closer to their fantasies. Some girls let them get closer than others. *I know you're anxious to get there, but just hold on...that part is coming up.* Most of the early showgirls had the heart, but a few never got it. They faded away to picket-fenced houses with two kids and a dog pretty quickly. That might have been the American Dream for most people in the '50s, but not for most showgirls. One of the girls who never got the heart was Jeannette Russell, the Brazilian beauty who stood still with me on that first nude engagement. She preferred ugly men, and her objective in Vegas was to find a crappy-looking guy who would be grateful and make her feel beautiful. She found her Prince Ugly soon after our first Vegas engagement and built her American Dream. Go figure.

A showgirl gets dressed up every night and knows she's going to a party, and she can hardly wait to get there—show after show, night after night. The jewelry and feathered costumes, the lights and glitter—they build the heart of a show-girl. But it's a two-way deal...us and you. It really just comes down to nice, easy-to-understand passion. You want us, and we let you believe you're going to have us. Our passion is even simpler. We want it all.

Vegas had it all for us. That's why some of us might leave for awhile until we'd get the itch that only Vegas could scratch and come prancing back! Vegas has always been a curious place to people. Living as a showgirl in the city that is not like any other city in the world was even more intriguing to our tourists.

There's a question that's a given: For 50 years, Vegas visitors have asked me, "Do people really live in Vegas?" Yes, we really do. Off the Strip, our town is just like your town. We have schools and churches and dry cleaners. They probably look the same as they do in any city in the country. Well, not exactly. Our grocery stores and car washes have slot machines.

Showgirl-specific questions back then were, "Does that thing hurt?" (Only a woman would dare ask this, and "that thing" was a G-string.) Hurt? Not so much—you start to get a permanent trench in your ass to hold the string. (Once I had the trench in my butt, it was a shame not to use it. Maybe that's why, to this day, I still only wear G-strings.) Wearing them was one thing, but shaving every day to make sure that everything was "nice and neat" was not delightful. (Whenever I'd say this to some woman, her husband would get an immediate "I'll-be-glad-to-help-you-with-that" look. America is a wonderful place. There are nice guys from every state always willing to lend a helping hand.)

The more typical tourist question for a showgirl was, "What do you do all day?" I thought that was pretty funny the first time I heard it. *Hey, Steve from Cleveland, do you think we walk around with all these feathers on all day? Or, maybe you're expecting (hoping) to hear tales of orgies in the sand? Or, do you just want to hang with us?*

Just what did showgirls do all day? Did we ever come out in the daylight, or were we the first celebrity vampires?

You've already gotten a peek into my showgirl world from 7:00 p.m. to 2:00 a.m. What about the rest of the time? Were we like regular people after work? Go home, kick off our shoes, and pop a beer? Not exactly. *Come on, I'll let you hang out with me. You might have fun. At the least, you might like to watch.*

A Showgirl's Wild Ride

Money-Making Fun: After the Last Show to 2:00 a.m....or 6:00 a.m.

The last show is over, except for those ball-busting third shows on Saturdays. (*I mean the balls of our feet. What were you thinking?*) Most nights after the last show, we "mixed," which was considered a part of the showgirl job. It may not have been on the job description (yeah, like we had job descriptions), but I made more money mixing than I did on stage, so I figured I was working and it was worth the "overtime" to stay until 2:00 a.m.

Mixing was really straightforward. When the last show ended, we weren't supposed to slink out the back door and go home. It was our job to keep the high-rollers in the casino laying their chips down on the tables. This was the time of night when the high-rollers got to believe that the showgirls wanted them as much as they wanted us, just because they were drooling after us. Yeah, sure we did. We drooled over them handing over chips for us to gamble with and to hoard.

Before the big shows, like the Folies and Casino de Paris, opened the mixing rule applied to both the showgirls and the dancers. The bosses wanted to make sure all their customers had their egos stroked with the attention of their lovelies, and it took all of us to do that. When the stages got bigger, however, so did the cast of both dancers and showgirls, which meant that the dancers no longer had to face more hours of standing around the casino after they had danced their hearts out in two back-to-back shows. Many of the dancers were shorter than the showgirls—5'5" to 5'8" was about average back then—and most of them were cute little things. In fact, in the early days at the Flamingo, El Rancho, and the Sahara, they used to call dancers the "pony line" because they looked like a herd of little prancing ponies. When the cast was large enough to let some girls go home, it was the dancers that were allowed to get home to their families. I'd like to think it was empathy for the hard work they'd put in, but it was likely also because they were more athletic looking than we were. Sound strange? Nowadays, athletic is desirable. Back then...not so much. In the '50s, who wanted a "bumpy road to heaven" down a dancer's washboard abs when you could think about sliding down our well-oiled bellies?

Well...about that "sliding down our well-oiled bellies." Maybe sometimes for some of the girls, but mixing was all about fantasy, and making money standing up.

It was easy to work the entire casino while you were mixing in those days. There were no mega-casinos—no MGM Grand Casino that's bigger than every town in Wyoming. Mixing in our casinos back then was like going to a house party. There were usually four craps tables and maybe six blackjack tables right off the showroom, with the slot machines lined up around the edges. (Now you have to walk three miles to get back to the tables after a show. How dumb is that? The Mob at least knew where their money was coming from. Get those people off their butts and standing around the craps table as fast as possible!)

Unless it was a really slow night, the high-rollers were plentiful and easy to spot. Our standard was to go to the lounge and join them for drinks. What we did after our "few drink minimum" was up to us. There were two kinds of mixing: meeting, greeting, drinking, and maybe gambling with our new "friends," and chip-hustling hooking. There were only a few showgirls who regularly engaged in the "hooking" activities and they were usually "hotel-approved" and on call for the high-rollers. (The Mob definitely did not encourage the "profession" of hooking by non-approved girls, and those girls were usually escorted out of the lounge. If there were to be any extra favors spread around, the bosses needed to control who was spreading what and with whom!)

Of course, we didn't just want to drink or stand around watching while our admirers played, we wanted to gamble too. A showgirl didn't gamble with her own money though, unless she was a real idiot. She'd get $100 to $400 in chips from the roller—some to play with and some to "put away." And I mean literally put away. We'd stick some of the chips in our bustier like we were putting showgirl mojo on them. No mojo…those chips were just getting comfortably warmed up until we could get to the cage to turn the smaller chips into larger ones (fewer to tuck away) or cash them in for real money. Sometimes we'd hide the real money, but more often, we'd pull out a pre-addressed, stamped envelope (that we kept in the cashier cages) and mail the money home to ourselves. With the "un-warmed" chips, we'd gamble for a few hours. If we won, it was casino courtesy to offer the original stake back. If we lost, oh well…

A chip-hustling hooker added extra dimensions to this up-close-and-personal-with-your-fantasy routine. One of the extras was that she'd also screw the high-roller for (usually)

$200. I could never figure out why this was a good deal. Why earn $200 for getting in bed with one of them when you can keep smiling, make him feel like Marlon Brando or Cary Grant, and play for free? (I was Cary Grant's girlfriend. Believe me— not one of them was Cary Grant. Most were closer to Wally Cox.) I've won more than $4,000 in a "mixing" night, so let's do the math: $200 for getting sweated on in a hotel room, or potentially $4,000 for drinks and laughter in the casino. You could buy a new car for four grand then! Staying upright for the mixing was a lot smarter deal.

There were all kinds of ways to get out of sleeping with the Wally Coxes. I remember one night at the Tropicana when I had won a bundle with my mixing chips. My guy finally said, "Let's go to my room." Only in your dreams, buddy. But I said, "Sure, but let's get a drink in the lounge first."

As I figured we'd find, there was a booth of four hookers there, just waiting for the next hookup. I asked my Wally Cox which one he liked. He immediately got into that question! He figured I was putting together a threesome. He took some time to carefully look over the "menu."

When my guy made his pick, I sent him to his room, took his extra room key over to the girl and said, "He wants to fuck you. I'll give you $200 now, and you make sure he's happy. And do NOT ask for any more money. If you ask for more, I'll find out, and you'll never see another John again, ever! If you do what you're supposed to and keep your mouth shut, except for when you're supposed to keep it full, then I'll give you another $200 tomorrow night."

With those two "lovebirds" taken care of, I went back to the tables. The next day, I heard from both of them. He was happy, she was happy (and got another $200 from me), and I was happy. Applause all around!

Another difference in chip-hustling hooking instead of mixing was that the hustler would sometimes take (or let the high-roller go) to another casino. Really a dumb move! That was the unspoken, no-exceptions rule all over town: "Do not take them out of the casino!" Like the Mob bosses weren't going to notice a big spender walking out the door? Those guys could smell money coming in or going out at 100 yards!

But, even if it was a slow night with no high-rollers to bank us at the tables, it didn't mean the party didn't go on. If we were already dressed to kill, we loved to catch the other lounge shows like Louie Prima, Ike and Tina Turner, Rowan and Martin, and Shecky Greene. We'd cap that off with hours of dancing at the Thunderbird and then stop in at Foxy's Delicatessen for chocolate éclairs and fried wontons. *A "healthy living tip for you," which is probably the only one you'll ever hear from me! If anyone ever tells you that you eat like a showgirl— it's time to back it down a little.*

If it was a 70-degree, no-wind, perfect Vegas night, we'd get on our motorcycles and chase rabbits in the desert (where New York New York is now.) If we were really energetic, we'd go home, change clothes, grab a big breakfast, and be at Bonnie Springs Ranch in Red Rock to ride horses at sunrise. Except for playing cowboys in Red Rock, though, whatever else we did, we wanted to be home by sunrise. No vampire stuff—we just looked really crappy by 6:00 a.m.!

One more exception to the sunrise rule was when we'd go to Lake Mead. If we had access to a boat (usually from some gambler or celebrity entertainer) a bunch of showgirls and boy dancers would drive down to Lake Mead about 2:00 a.m. We'd sleep on board the boat until the sun came up, and then we'd go water skiing in the nude. There was nothing too sexy about it. We just weren't allowed to have tan lines or tattoos or pierce any miscellaneous body parts. The only way to avoid the dreaded tan lines on Lake Mead was to ski and swim in the tiniest G-string you had. I wonder what went through the minds of the early-morning tourists on Lake Mead when they saw us on the water. Yeah, I wonder...

Crash: 6:00 a.m. to 1:00 p.m.
Sleep! Unless, there was another damn publicity job to do.

We didn't get too excited about showing up for promotional appearances because they happened at unholy times of the day, like before noon. It screwed up our whole night-before fun and made us face the daylight...in the day! But there we were, posing and smiling, handing out trophies for race cars or horses or some other damn fool thing, or cutting the ribbon on some new something in town.

I still have a memo from Harvey Diederich, one of the most admired men in Vegas and the Tropicana publicist who was responsible for building the early branding of the Trop as the "Tiffany's of the Strip." The memo asks four of us to meet in front of the Trop for a shoot at "...8:45 a.m.—that's in the morning—Friday, March 11." Harvey knew he had to call out "in the morning." The meeting was for pictures of the official opening of the last leg of the Las Vegas–Los Angeles Freeway. Now, that's hot. Not. But Harvey didn't let anything happen in Vegas without a Tropicana showgirl in the camera's eye. (Like Mayor Oscar Goodman, who will probably have to have his showgirls surgically removed from his body when he leaves office. Like Harvey, Mayor Goodman doesn't miss a chance to draw publicity for Vegas, and what better draw than a couple of gorgeous girls?) I finally told Harvey that unless the opening was something better than a can of tuna, I wasn't going out at eight in the morning! But he kept booking me, and I kept showing up.

Another pain-in-the-butt requirement that would cut our precious sleeping time short was rehearsal, if someone—anyone—had screwed up on stage the night before. It wasn't just the "screwer-upper" that was expected to show up for these rehearsals—it was all of us screw-ees too! The entire line had to be there at 11:00 a.m. and go through all the numbers until we were letter-perfect. We also had to do rehearsals every time a new girl would join us, to make sure she was in sync and looked like the "one" showgirl we were all supposed to be.

We often made mistakes in the rehearsals that we would never have made "live." We didn't have the audience and the lights and the excitement to keep us on point. That meant that sometimes the rehearsals would last a lot longer than they should have. Usually just long enough to screw up the rest of our day. Royal pain in the butt!

Regular Girl Time: 1:00 p.m. to 7:00 p.m.

This was the most "regular" part of our day. This was shopping, apartment-cleaning, letter-writing, errand-running time. We did what everybody else did in our spare time, except maybe for making G-strings. If we had rhinestone-studded G-strings as part of our costume, they were supplied, but if we wore skirts, G-strings were still a basic part of our "uniforms," but you couldn't actually buy them anywhere during those years. So, we made our own G-strings and then attached them to flesh-colored tights that had the elastic tops cut off. I liked to use fun fabric with ducks and flags and kittens. Who cared? No one ever saw them underneath the elaborate costumes— except maybe my water skiing buddies and the first-up tourists at Lake Mead.

By 5:00 p.m., it was time to grab your evening clothes for the night, put on five pairs of eyelashes, and run off to work. I looked like I had small furry animals in the middle of my face for years. We could afford to cut the timing to get to work really close back then. We didn't fight traffic on the Strip. Even though the Strip was just a two-lane road, we were never more than five minutes away. And when we got to the hotel, we didn't have to park a mile away in the Employee Parking Lot and take a shuttle, with the housekeepers and dealers and every other employee, like they do today. We just pulled up near the door into the parking lot that everyone, including the customers, used, and there we were...ready to get ready.

Actually, there was a down side to the just-barely-not-a-desert-anymore town we lived in then. Although we didn't have gridlock and eight-story parking ramps four blocks away from the hotel, we did have desert critters in the parking lot to contend with. More than once, we had to wear fishing boots to get in from our car because of the big, ugly black bugs that would swarm all over the parking lot! And you didn't want to walk without a flashlight at night because you didn't want to stumble across snakes or lizards, or desert rats. Sometimes we felt like pioneer women—only without the wagons and the ugly, cotton bonnets.

Once we got inside, the first order of business was getting on the rest of the makeup. The standard for all showgirls was Max Factor #6N pancake makeup that we liberally applied with a damp sponge. Plenty of black eyeliner drew even more attention to the five pairs of eyelashes—as if they weren't obvious enough! We used dark brown lip liner and filled in the lines with deep, sexy red lipstick that came in a jar. A good dose of Mehron lip gloss would complete the look. It was all about big in those days—big eyes, big lips, big tits.

Then it was time to get assembled. We'd lay out all the accessories for the night's quick changes. We had dressers to help us in and out of feathered wings and elaborate hoop skirts, but we changed the jewelry, shoes, gloves, and other goodies ourselves. Sometimes all this undressing and dressing had to happen in three minutes! For some numbers, we'd have more changing time backstage while we were waiting for some damn monkey act to get over. For those down times, we'd lay out our library books, knitting, or Barron's. (Working on investment strategies was a popular backstage pastime. You'd think that on a couple 100 a week we wouldn't make enough to invest. Remember mixing and mailing the money home? Hello-o-o-o, Mr. Stockbroker!)

While we were organizing all our accessories, we'd work on warming up our bra "parts" and any fancy G-strings we had to put on first that night. It didn't matter what the temperature was in the dressing room, those rhinestones were always cold! We'd hang them off our dressing table lights to keep from getting frostbite on our most marketable body parts.

While the rhinestoned parts were warming, we started with our heads and worked our way down. First, all the hair had to get pulled up and pinned down so the headpieces, and sometimes wigs, would cover most of it. We all needed to look the same on stage. No blond bangs sticking out, no Shirley Temple curls just because we thought they were cute. Collectively, we were just one girl.

We'd get our tall headdresses or sparkly, tight caps on and then get strapped in, hooked up, or pinned into the fancy, heavy, custom-made costumes. We sure couldn't do that by ourselves. We stood in just our G-strings, mesh tights, heels, and jewelry while the dressers swarmed around us in their boring little smocks, like nannies fussing over spoiled children.

The rhinestone-covered or feather skirts were usually laid out on the floor, and we stepped into them and got hooked or snapped or pinned—whatever it took to keep the skirts on. Bra-fitting was a lot like passing a kidney stone—not easy, not pleasant, and not as fast as you hoped. The "bras" were usually cup-less pieces of angle iron and rhinestones that were fastened around our necks with a chain. Finally, the dressers strapped on our wings or 20-pound velvet capes or huge (real) furs. In between numbers, we'd do it again! Half-naked showgirls trying to change gloves and jewelry, the dressers running after us saying, "Hold on, your G-string is crooked," trying to pin us back into a "bra" that just lost a snap, or stitching up a hole in our hose on the fly. I'm talking chaos here!

But it all came together, at least most of the time. And then we were showgirls—showing it all!

Getting the Showgirl Groove On

"Why can't you just stay in one place for awhile? You need to settle down! You keep running your ass back and forth to Vegas to parade around half-naked! Just wait, one of these days, you're going to fall in love and want to get pregnant. You think you're going to be a showgirl with your belly out to here?" My sister Barbara, who was sitting there with her "belly out to here" was ragging on me about getting my show girl groove on, again and again and again.

I never intended to get pregnant. I planned to be a show-girl, or a model or an actress or maybe a kept housewife (without the kids), for my whole life. I was in love with my life and meant to keep it that way. (I hadn't really seen far enough ahead to envision my driving the damn limo instead of sitting in the back. Hmmm…that part didn't exactly work out just the way I thought it would. That's what happens when you don't have a Life Plan A, I guess.)

I certainly didn't have any maternal instincts, and if my biological clock was ever ticking, I must have had a pillow over it because I never heard it. I had already gotten sick of taking care of those four sisters who kept on coming, and I still remember those ugly maternity clothes my mother seemed to be wearing for my whole life. They were horrible things that looked like camping tents with bands underneath them to keep her belly hidden. Not for me!

I remember asking my mother once how those babies got in there. (I wanted to know what to avoid.) She said it was a seed. Not long after I heard that, I was helping our maid make my mother's bed. I saw some little black seeds in the bed. My mother liked to eat in bed, and they must have been poppy seeds, but they looked like baby seeds to me. I flipped those things off the sheets and stomped them to dust! If that was another baby coming, I intended to stop it right then!

Lying about my age, and definitely not telling my Catholic-to-the-core mother, I had signed up for the birth control pill trials in L.A. not long after they started in 1956. I think I was the first in line to get my prescription. (Yep, I lied about my age for that gig too.) Getting pregnant and giving up Vegas and my lifestyle in Hollywood…not then and not ever!

From the time I was 13-years-old, I knew I had to be a showgirl. Becoming a showgirl was validation that I was no longer the ugly kid in school. And when I say "ugly," I'm not making it up.

When I was 12, I asked my mother, "Did you know your kids would grow up looking like me? Why did you have any if you knew they'd be ugly?"

"Oh my dear, you're not ugly," she said. "Well, maybe your nose, but we'll fix that when you're 18. And maybe that hair, but we can probably get that fixed too. And hold in your stomach." I think my mother's almost constant pregnant state cause her to be obsessed with a flat stomach.

"Do you see that Mexican woman over there—the fat one? Hold in your stomach or that's what you're going to look like." I heard that from my mother more than a few times!

The first step in my transformation was to fix my Brillo-pad hair. When I was 16, I had finally worn my mother down with my incessant nagging, which resulted in a trip to Westmore's beauty parlor in Hollywood to get the kinks out of the ball of wire on my head. It took all day, but I didn't care. I was on the quest to "stop being ugly!" Besides, I was distracted by some of the high-profile Hollywood clientele that were coming in for their beauty treatments. I remember seeing Jane Russell getting a pedicure. She was really gorgeous, but did she ever have ugly toes! I just kept staring at them. To this day, whenever I see red polish, I think about Jane Russell's ugly feet.

Anyway, they coated my head with white Vaseline stuff, and combed and combed and combed. It took all day! I fell asleep twice while this was going on, but when I came out of there, my hair was straight! That was a life-changing experience for me.

Getting my Lebanese schnoz cut down to size, however, was my top priority. My mother and I went to several different doctors, but I hated them all. I wanted the perfect doctor who could make the magical nose that would transform me into a walking, breathing work of art. I was window shopping down Hollywood Boulevard one Saturday when I saw it. I saw The Nose! It was attached to a gorgeous tall girl who looked like an angel. She had the nose I had to have: my perfect little nose.

I followed the gorgeous girl for a few blocks and was almost glued to her side as she went into Chandler's Shoe Store. She must have known I was stalking her, but she probably wasn't too worried about a gawky, skinny girl with a big nose. I sat down next to her in Chandler's and tried to find the courage to actually speak to her. I didn't want to come right out and ask about her nose, but I couldn't take my eyes off it. While we were talking, I found out she was a showgirl at Ciro's in Hollywood. Amazing! (It must have been an omen.)

I finally asked, "Who fixed your nose?"

"God did, honey. I was born with this nose. But my sister had an ugly nose like yours, and Dr. Harold Holden fixed hers." (I took no offense about the comparison to her sister's nose. She was right. Anyone could see that my nose had to go.) The girl gave me Dr. Holden's number, and I raced home to break the good news. I had found The Doctor who could make The Nose!

A few days later, my mother and I were sitting in Dr. Holden's office. He looked like The One—white hair, white mustache, with a TV-doctor smile. I showed him my dog-eared magazine pictures of the nose I wanted, and he said I shouldn't have it. He advised that with my big eyes and big lips, I'd look like a Pomeranian with that little nose I showed him. But, he promised me that he could fix me up with the right one, and he did. Check that off the make-Lisa-beautiful list! (Dr. Holden still owes me a lot of referral money! He got to fix the noses of my mother, my Aunt Emma, Eva from Vegas, and my best friend, Gerri. And who says I can't sell?)

It was meant to be. I had to be a showgirl or an actress, or both, when I grew up. Either one seemed like a better fit for me than being a nurse, a teacher, or a nun. Those were Immaculate Heart High School's "occupations of choice" for us. Every year during Vocation Week, those three thrill-of-a-lifetime options were presented, usually by the same tired and nasty-looking nurse, teacher, or nun, year after year. Maybe they could only find one of each who was willing to talk about their boring lives. Or maybe they just all looked the same. Whatever…that wasn't going to be me. I didn't particularly have anything against any of those jobs for someone else, just not for Loretta Malouf.

Showgirls were beautiful, and I wanted to be beautiful. Actresses got all the attention, and I definitely liked attention. My classmates and neighbors in Los Feliz, California, came from acting families or were already famous stars, and my personal heroes were showgirls. I wanted to be like the angel in Chandler's Shoes with The Nose, the showgirls I saw in Vegas when my parents went there to gamble, and our neighbor Hope Dare.

Hope Dare had been a Ziegfeld Follies girl, and she was married to a gangster who owned Good Time Ice Cream. It didn't get much better than that for a Heroine's Resume. All the other kids on our street liked the ice cream that she handed out whenever we went to play with her two boys, but I liked looking at her. She looked like a magical princess with red (not Brillo pad) hair and reddish brown false eyelashes that looked like furry spider's legs. I remember her silky print dress and the matching topaz and diamond ring, earrings, and brooch she often wore. And I remember her legs. They were so shapely and smooth, unlike my skinny, knock-kneed legs. I wanted to be like Hope Dare.

But if being a showgirl in Vegas was so great, why didn't I stay around permanently after that first gig? Why all the to-ing and fro-ing for 11 years? For openers, I had stuff—interesting stuff—going on in Hollywood, besides having a couple of husbands and a few love affairs, that I had to squeeze into those 11 years. I was modeling, acting, getting divorced, getting married, getting laid. No moss was growing under my ass. Besides those distractions, sometimes I just needed to remember that Vegas didn't imitate life. Vegas imitated…only Vegas. I did have it all as a showgirl, but "all" can taint you real fast. You start to believe that everybody downs a fifth of Scotch every night, and all girls go to dinner with the expectation of a new diamond bracelet. There was too much booze, too much partying, too much not real. I needed to come up for air once in awhile. (*Like today, when you start to think the ceiling in Caesars Forum is really the sky—go home!*)

Another thing that messed with reality was that the days all ran together. Back then, the showrooms were never "dark." We performed seven nights a week, two shows a night, and, too often, three shows on Saturday. We were supposed to get three days off a month, but if any of the girls were out sick, our off days got rolled over to the next month (not exactly rolled—they limped along with our aching feet!). Sometimes I just needed to get real, or get laid (Vegas wasn't great for that, I was too tired), or I just wanted to get back to L.A. to live a "normal" life in Hollywood for awhile. (See how screwed up I was then? I thought Hollywood was normal!)

Walking around Vegas wearing five pairs of eyelashes when it was 110 fucking degrees was also an incentive to retreat to California periodically. Only the devil and his agents can live at that temperature forever.

It was mostly my Hollywood commitments that kept me from letting my showgirl heart beat for over a year after my first Riviera show. *Yes, I'm going to tell you about Lisa's Wild Ride in Hollywood. If you just can't wait, flip over to Chapter Five, and then come back. I'll wait for you here.*

As soon as I had an open spot in my life, the request for TV show appearances dried up for awhile, and my husband (whichever husband I had at the time) continued to piss me off, I high-tailed it back to Vegas. I did a 30-day run in the George Gobel show at the Riviera, but I was really excited when I got to strut my stuff in the Folies Bergere at the Tropicana on that big stage with those great costumes. Well, at least great furs, feathers, and jewelry. The cost of the feathers alone for the Folies was $69,000. And that was 50 years ago! (I used one of those cool calculators that figures how much that's equivalent to today. That would be like spending $508,000 today for feathers! Any idea how many naked ostriches that meant?) With $69,000 in feathers, we all looked like ducks in heat. It was great!

As you probably know, the Folies was a topless show, which meant the most lustful applause, more pay for me, and a bigger herd of high-rollers in the casino. I hate writing that "…the Folies was…" I wish it could be "…the Folies is…" But it's gone—closed just a few months short of its 50th Anniversary in 2009. All of us "originals" treated its closing like a death in the family, and when we get together today, the talk goes quickly to the Folies. I'm glad I helped the Trop "gift me" with some of the jewelry when I left the Folies. It will come in handy if (when) I decide to join that over-70s production number.

Going back to Vegas for that second time, and every other time I showed up there during the next decade, the one thing that wasn't a problem for me was getting a spot in the shows I wanted. I just called up my favorite Mob boss, Carl Cohen, and the next day I'd have a contract. I worked all over the Strip in those years. I went from the Riviera to the Tropicana to the Dunes to the Trop again, the Sands, the Trop again, the Riviera, the Frontier, the Trop again. I have a hard time remembering just exactly when I worked where. (I told you this wasn't a history book.) It's true that "if you can remember the '60s, you weren't there." Well, I was there, and although I do remember (most) of what I did, I'm just not really sure what year I did…whatever I was doing. Oh well.

There was one minor issue that second time I played Las Vegas. I didn't really know what a showgirl did on stage. I didn't have the walk, and I wasn't sure how to deal with all those feathers. I needed to perfect my on-stage showgirl atti-tude. Remember, my spotlight experience was standing still. How the hell do they walk around in those costumes without breaking something? Details… how tedious.

My guardian angel when I returned to Vegas was Ida Mercier. She was breathtakingly beautiful, elegant and sophisticated, and I was her "charity case." She took hold-still-nude Lisa and showed her how to be walk-around-topless Lisa.

If you want to learn the showgirl strut at home, you need to put together some equipment first, and then I'll tell you what Ida told me. If you're a guy, you might want to get your girl to try this, unless you really feel the need to do it yourself. I suggest you wait until you're alone then. Your hunting buddies may never share a cabin with you again.

You'll need:
- ❖ 20 pounds of books
- ❖ Two bathrobe sashes, but not some skimpy silk things; get out your after-the-shower terry cloth robes and pull off the ties
- ❖ A wide leather belt
- ❖ A rag mop with a stiff handle
- ❖ Your little brother's (or your kid's) backpack; fill it with 20 pounds of flour
- ❖ A five-pound sack of sugar
- ❖ A heavy bedspread
- ❖ The highest pair of heels you have

Got it all? Okay, now strap the books on your head with your bathrobe sash, and put the leather belt around your waist. Stick the mop in the belt running up your back so the raggedy mop ends are about 12 inches over your head. Run the other tie through the top of the sugar sack and tie it around your neck. Get the backpack on and step into your high heels. Then wrap the bedspread around you. Now you have on the headdress, the wings, the furs, and the sexy shoes that make your legs go right up to your butt. Ready? Now we're going to walk.

The first thing Ida told me was, "Take control of those clothes. Don't let them wear you. It's survival out there. You're packing over 50 pounds of costume!" *Okay…take control. Tell it, "You will not beat me. I own all of you, and you will move with me like my second skin." Really heavy second skin. You can do it! Can you hear the applause yet?*

Ida said, "The walk starts with the look in your eyes. Hold your head back, and before you make a move, give the audience the look that says, 'Don't you wish you were with me instead of that ugly, old bitch sitting next to you?' Keep that head up unless you want to bend like a pretzel and fall flat on your face. Never, never, never look down—if just one time, you tip your head, it's all over, girl. Then smile and smile and smile—but do not laugh. If you do, your tits will jiggle. Showgirls tits do not jiggle!"

Okay, got it? Hold both arms straight out and glide for 10 minutes. No, don't tip over! Now prance for 10 minutes. I know, I know…your knees hurt. Just woman-up and tough it out. Now run up and down a flight of stairs a few times. Then take all that crap off and lay down for awhile. Or, be a showgirl—wait two or three minutes and do it again.

Ida also warned me to be careful of the other girls when I went from the Riviera to the Trop. She said they'd be mean and pick on me because I was the new girl and I was taking someone else's spot. It didn't matter if the other girls even liked the one that was fired to open a spot for the new one. It was a matter of principle. Ida told me about epic catfights that sometimes occurred backstage and warned me to protect my face. Scratches could be covered up with makeup, but black eyes took forever to disguise! I found out real fast that she was warning me for good reason!

The crap they pulled on the new girls went from just irritating to dangerous. With 10 costume changes a show, you had to lay out your jewelry and gloves and shoes just perfectly to make the quick switches. Gloves and jewelry were laid out in drawers in the exact order you needed them. The shoes waited for you on a shelf right above the drawers, and your wigs and headdresses were right over the shoes they went with. Everything had to be right there, ready. So, just to mess with the rookies, the other girls would mix up the order or hide your gloves or cut the snaps off—pain-in-the-butt, kid stuff.

One night, the razzing jumped from middle-school-stupid to in-your-face ugly. Two of the girls had wedged their makeup chairs against mine so I couldn't get up. I pushed hard, and my chair crashed into (I'll call her) Eva and knocked the comb out of her hand. She jumped up and shoved me away from her. Now, you can call me whatever you want, but don't be laying your hands on me. She yelled, "You can just pick that comb up for me!" Nope, that was not going to happen. I got a good handful of Eva's hair, and we went at it. Legs, arms, and chairs were flying. It was the Clash of the Titans—showgirl style.

I gave Eva a good shot to the stomach and said, "You can pick that comb up with your teeth." The backstage guards had come running when they heard the commotion, but it was over before they had to step in. Eva and I have been good friends ever since. Eva was the unofficial leader of the glitter pack and packed a helluva punch, let me tell you! She had tested me the way veterans took stock of the new girls, and I had passed. I was worthy of being one of them. It wasn't glamorous, but it was the showgirl "rite of passage."

Ida continued to be a friend throughout our Vegas times together, although I didn't really know that much about her personally. Actually, no one did at the time. We knew she was married to a cop in L.A., but she didn't talk about him, or anyone else, too often. Years later, we found out why she seemed to disappear for a few days at a time, and why she didn't bore us to death backstage with cop-husband talk.

It seems that Ida was "well-connected" with Sid Wyman, a highly-regarded casino owner and boss who had originally started as a bookmaker with the St. Louis–Cleveland Mob. Sid was a tall, heavy-set man who was loved by his employees and customers and, while maybe not loved, was certainly respected by the poker players whose money he won regularly. The man played some serious poker! (As a testimony to the respect for the man and for the poker player, during Sid's funeral in 1978, all gaming play at the Dunes was halted for two minutes in his honor. Two minutes translates to a lot of money left on the table to honor one of Vegas' finest!)

We eventually found out that Ida had a scary side deal going on with Sid. She was his money-runner for the Dunes Hotel and took the cash from the various Mob-owned casinos in Vegas to St. Louis or Cleveland or wherever it was supposed to end up. I remember seeing her with a large, beat-up satchel one day and figured she'd bought the world's ugliest makeup bag. Damn. I'm glad I didn't try to take some eyeliner out of it. The Mob didn't care who took their money or why.

Messing with those boys—not a good thing to do.

Did you notice the pixie haircut? Look higher up.

THREE

Working with the "Boys"

Who's Afraid of the Big Bad Mob?

"Why can't my cousins from Las Vegas come to my birthday party? Aren't they even going to send presents?"

I complained to my mother about an oversight by my flashy "relatives" who had obviously forgotten that they had a cousin in L.A. who was turning 13. For years, I thought all the boys in the Mob were related to us. In keeping with old-world Lebanese manners, any friends of our parents were our "aunts" or "uncles," and their kids were our "cousins." It took me a long while to figure out that they weren't really my relatives. I guess that's why I never got birthday presents. I got screwed early on by the Mob.

You can't even think about the beginnings of Vegas without including the Mob. Vegas and the Mob, they went together like boobs and glitter. Most of the girls in the shows were either oblivious to the Mob bosses or just steered clear and didn't know any of them. I wasn't sure why they shied away from the "boys," though. I sure didn't. I wasn't afraid of the big, bad Mob; I was attracted to their power. (I've always been drawn to strong men, like a moth to a flame—a sparkly, long-legged, fun-loving moth.)

Besides all the power they wielded, the boys were good to all of their employees. And their rules were really simple to understand: You do the boys right and they'll take care of you. But if you cross them, you might get a one-way ride to the desert.

Going to Vegas with my parents when I was a kid, I had already met many of the boys, and I certainly had nothing against them. Like any other "fraternal organization," some of the Mob bosses were good guys and some were real bastards. So what? In Hollywood and in business everywhere, there are nice guys and there are real bastards. Okay, maybe the assholes in corporate America don't have you shot in the desert, but they're still assholes. And their rules are a lot harder to understand!

I'll share my memories of some of the Mobsters who wove in and out of my life. For a complete picture of what it was like then, see my friend Steve Fischer's book, *When the Mob Ran Vegas*. He covers it all! *When you pick up the book, check out that kick-ass showgirl on the back cover. Yep, that's me...Lisa Malouf Medford.*

In the early days of Vegas, we figured out real fast which boys to trust and which ones were like pimples before the Prom. Whenever we'd hear "Johnny Marshall" being paged, we'd figure that somebody was going to take an extended desert vacation—like, forever. Johnny was the "take care of the problem" guy—the Mob's hit man when I first went to Vegas. Johnny wasn't the name he was born with though. I don't know if I ever heard his real name back then. If I did, I had forgotten it, as I carefully explained several times to the FBI when they questioned me about "Johnny Marshall." But now I know who he was. He was Marshall Caifano, who was the most successful (from the Mob's perspective) hit man in the country. (Rumor has it that he was "credited" with 50 hits! Busy guy.) It's amazing how even thinking about the most scary-ass guy in Vegas can mess with your head! (I guess the FBI doesn't need me to call them back with the name, though. They figured it out too.) I do remember what Johnny looked like though: hunky Italian with freaky, Mr. Universe arms bulging out of his golf shirts. He looked like The Hulk, except not green. Johnny was good-looking alright, but he was also the stuff that nightmares are made of. The word was that he had a real thing for using a blowtorch—and he wasn't doing plumbing. When Johnny Marshall walked into a room, everybody got the willies.

After the El Rancho Vegas burned down in 1960, Marshall was replaced by Johnny Roselli as the hit man of choice. I developed a real prejudice against the name "Johnny." (Wish I would have remembered that when I was going with the singer Johnny Rivers many years later. He didn't go around wasting people, but he sure pissed away a bunch of my time!)

Through all my Vegas years, I just didn't need to know or care about who was stealing from the Mob. Besides, if they were stupid enough to think the Mob wouldn't catch them with their hands in the money slots on the tables, then maybe they needed killing. The rules just weren't that complicated.

I do want you to know about Carl Cohen, though. He was the casino manager at the Sands, my favorite Mob boss, and my dear friend for all of my Vegas years. Carl Cohen was a teddy-bear sweetheart: over six feet tall and usually north of 250 pounds, with gorgeous, bright blue eyes. I would call Carl first when I arrived in Vegas and he'd ask me where I wanted to work. Whatever show I named, he made it happen with one phone call. While I was working, Carl and I would meet at the Garden Room Coffee Shop at the Sands, usually twice a week for breakfast, just to keep in touch. (The Garden Room had the best food in town. I can still taste the grilled cheese with juicy beefsteak tomatoes.)

I remember during one breakfast, a maitre d' came up and whispered in Carl's ear. I knew it wasn't, "You might want to try the new recipe for Hollandaise sauce," from the expression on Carl's face. You didn't really want to hear what the Mob bosses were talking about. You just never knew when you might be expected to repeat that to some attorney, which was a no-no. So, I leaned way back in my chair and tried to be out of that conversation. Carl replied to the maitre d', "I'll take care of it," and I thought, "Whoops. Somebody's in deep doggie doo-doo tonight."

Carl turned to me and said, "Let's go for a ride." What? Not me! What did I do wrong? Why am I getting dumped in the desert? I figured I was dead. "Go for a ride" usually meant a one-way ride.

Instead of the desert, however, we went to the old jail downtown, where Carl bailed out a Mexican busboy who had been arrested for drunk driving. Carl gave the guy $100, talked to him like a father, warned him not to drink again, and told him to show up for work the next day. That was Carl. He was the best of the best of the casino bosses. The good ones protected their employees and treated them like family. But they were not only good-hearted; they were also shrewd. The employees knew things, so the Mob needed to keep them close. If a customer complained, the employee wasn't immediately fired. Not like today, when one complaining bitch who's falling-down drunk on comped cheap booze can get a hard-working cocktail waitress fired. In those days, the bosses just sent you over to another property. It didn't matter which hotel, because just a handful of the Mob owned them all.

Treating us like members of the family was how most of the Mob bosses treated their employees (except for a few of the rat bastards). I remember seeing the bosses come out to the floor on a slow night when the dealers were just standing at their tables, looking lonely and broke with no one to play with—making no money on those nights. More than once, I'd see Carl or Sid (Wyman) or one of the other good guys reach into the money slot at the table, pull out a bunch of bills, and tell the dealer to go home and take it easy. "Don't worry about it. They'll be coming in tomorrow. Tonight? Just put your feet up." Yeah, like **that** would happen today! After the Mob bosses moved out of Vegas (many to less luxurious accommodations in jail or in hiding somewhere), the employees weren't family any more. Hell, not even the customers were treated too well!

Without the Mob, Vegas just made too many rules. In the '80s, I was visiting in Vegas, and my sister Joanna and her boyfriend came in for a few days. I had told them, "Don't play the slot machines. Those are the worst odds in Vegas!"

Sure, what do I know? Joanna hit one of the first big progressive jackpots on the Strip. She put in $30 and won $345,000! I came in to meet them just as the bells starting going off, so I got caught in the "quarantine" along with them. It was nuts! We were there about 12 hours—couldn't leave the spot, couldn't play, couldn't do shit, while the casino checked every record in Joanna's and her boyfriend's entire lives. They went through police records, dental records, FBI records, IRS filings, and grade school report cards and then ran the video back about three dozen times. What a hassle! When you won with the Mob, you got paid. When you lost...you paid them. Easy.

Carl Cohen was the best of the great casino bosses—kind and generous and something of a prophet. On the other end of the good-guy spectrum was Gus Greenbaum, from the Chicago Mob and one of the owners of the Riviera. He was a nasty, nasty man. He told me that if I didn't sleep with him, I wouldn't have a job. I've kissed a lot of frogs looking for my prince, but I wasn't about to sleep with that slimy lizard. Naturally, I told Carl, who told me not to worry because, "He won't be bothering anyone for long." Two weeks later, Gus and his wife were found with their throats cut. Maybe Carl made a lucky guess?

Carl was not only my favorite casino boss, but just about everyone else's too, except for Frank Sinatra. Howard Hughes was tired of Sinatra's ego-fueled antics and cut off his credit line. Hughes owned the Sands, so he outranked Frank by a mile. Sinatra blamed Carl for getting cut off and confronted him in the Sands restaurant. After too-drunk Frank swore at him, nice easy-going Carl punched him in the face! With a bloody nose and missing two caps on his front teeth, Sinatra stormed out of the casino. (As the story goes, he drove a golf cart through the window. Wish I would have seen that!) In that same day, everyone in Vegas heard about the fight. We didn't need texting then. Great news like that would spread faster than a Strip hooker's legs. There was much celebration in Vegas about Frank's take-down.

Vegas showed its approval, Vegas-style. Comedian Dick Martin had a red satin boxer's robe made for Carl with "The Man Who Slew the Dragon" on the back. He presented it to Carl in a formal ceremony accompanied by enthusiastic applause from all of us! Yep, there was joy in Mudville (the Sands actually) when Sinatra crossed the street to sign with Caesars Palace. Good! Let them deal with the asshole.

And what a real asshole he was. I remember playing black-jack at a table with Sinatra. Next to him was a good-looking, 30-something woman. Frank whispered something obviously disgusting to her, and she said she wasn't interested. He did it several times and was turned down more aggressively each time. Then when she wasn't looking, I saw Frank put his gold Dunhill lighter into the woman's purse. When he said something that must have been really rude, the woman said, "No way," and stood up to leave. As soon as she turned away from the table, Frank hollered, "Guard, guard! She stole my lighter. Arrest her." And they did. That was Sinatra.

Why am I talking about Sinatra in a section about the "boys"? You know why—he was a Mafia wanna-be. He had his nose so far up the Mob's butt, I don't know how he could breathe.

Most of the other Mob bosses were just "there," doing what they did and leaving us alone. We knew that Joe Agosto was "officially" the Tropicana Hotel Showroom Manager, but mostly he was in charge of skimming. Pretty easy to figure out when he was seldom in the showroom and instead hung out in the counting room. We just didn't pay that much attention to the boys' "affiliations"—didn't ask them if they belonged to the Moose Lodge, the Rotary Club, or the Mafia.

One stand-out memory is a "cross-over" for me, because it includes the Mob, a showgirl, and Hollywood (although the

Hollywood part came later.) In between shows one night, this conversation took place.

"Hey, Lisa, I need you to do something for me. There's a girl who needs to be trained to be a showgirl real fast or she's going to get her hooker ass run out of Vegas. This isn't my idea, but I need to do a favor for a friend. He'll be real unhappy if she's not on stage in three nights. I'll really appreciate it if you'd do this for me." While he was asking me this, Sid Wyman laid $3,000 in my hand. That was a no-brainer. For a grand a night, I'd try to turn the girl into whatever he wanted! One showgirl coming up—I'd be glad to help keep her hooker ass in Vegas!

I tucked the $3,000 into my bustier and hurried backstage to take my spot in the opening number of the second show that night. Damn. I said I could do this. I'd better be able to pull it off! At that time, we had 10 costume changes per show. Ten costumes meant 10 different numbers. What to wear when, how to get in and out of all the feathers, furs, jewelry, and headdresses in less than two minutes, where to stand, how to move—this is in the category of "don't try this at home." I've seen new showgirls fall flat on their asses trying to balance a 30-pound headdress. And I needed to teach her all this in three nights? I'd never taught someone else the routines. What if I failed? Well, I'd have to teach fast…and she'd better suck it all up. I wasn't afraid of Sid, but I sure as hell did not want to give back the $3,000 and disappoint the rest of the "boys"!

That's how I met Geri Marmor. *Doesn't ring a bell? You know who she was—Geri McGee Marmor* **Rosenthal**—*Lefty Rosenthal's wife?* Everyone met her in the 1995 film, *Casino,* when Sharon Stone played Ginger McKenna, who was modeled after Geri.

Robert De Niro played her husband, Frank "Lefty Rosenthal," and Joe Pesci was that slimy Tony "The Ant" Spilotro. *You don't remember* Casino*? Maybe you need to give this book to your dad—you just may be too young to be reading this!*

Thirty years before Sharon Stone's Geri Marmor, I gave Geri the coaching that made her a showgirl, that then made the Mob let her stay in Vegas, which allowed her to eventually marry Lefty Rosenthal. She went on to try to kill him (didn't work—crappy car bomb), and she eventually overdosed on alcohol, Valium, and cocaine (or so they say.)

I had heard about Geri Marmor from some of the other girls, but I hadn't met her before Sid asked for my (well-paid-for) help. She was one of those chip-hustler hookers I told you about, which is why some of the Mob wanted her gone. She was hustling, but she was also seeing Lefty Rosenthal and Tony Spilotro and... (Geri didn't let any grass grow under her ass). The rest of the Mob wanted her out, but Lefty wanted her in. So that's why Geri had to learn to be a showgirl. Putting this together, it only took me a few more minutes to understand why Sid was enlisting my help.

I met the needs-to-be-a-showgirl-fast after my first show the night after my conversation with Sid. Okay, at least she had showgirl looks. *Take a minute, close your eyes, and imagine this.* She's 28 years old; 5'8", lots of dark blonde tumbling hair, big breasts, long legs, round, luscious 1950s-style hips, and skin like a baby's butt. *Got the picture? Now, open your eyes and keep reading. I said...open them up now.*

I had something to work with. Sharon Stone played Geri like she was a loud, noisy drunk, but the Geri I knew in 1964 was quiet and laid-back, although she was a little stand-offish from the other girls. She was a "ghost." She didn't gossip (which was a showgirl's regular pastime) and never bragged, even though she sure could have. She was going with Lefty Rosenthal, and he was a big man in Vegas! Geri never talked about her personal life at all, which was really unusual in show-girl-speak. I didn't even know she had a daughter, Robin, when she arrived in Vegas. I only found out about Robin many, many years later. Geri kept herself and her daughter very hidden and protected.

I trained Geri on stage in between the shows and after the last show for three days. She picked it right up. She learned almost as fast as I did for my first time on-stage. (Well, almost.) She was serious about becoming a showgirl. I'm sure she knew she was getting run out of town, so she had to make this work. And she did!

The night Geri opened, she was flawless. She wore the huge furs, dazzling jewels, and long, bright feathers like she was born in them. She only worked as a showgirl for about a year, but when she did, she was damn good! But Geri never did have the heart of a showgirl; she only performed because she wanted to stay in Vegas. Geri was rarely seen in the casino and didn't do her mixing requirement. At the time, we had no idea that she was hotfooting it over to the Stardust as soon as she could rip off her pasties. We just thought it was Geri being ghostly. But the Stardust was where her boyfriend, Lefty, was the Casino Manager and the "Man of the Hour." Lefty Rosenthal was a good-looking, tall, blue-eyed devil who dressed like Tom Landry—a little different dresser than De Niro played him in *Casino*. Lefty didn't need to wear flashy suits. He was just pure class—nice, sexy class. He was "King of the Strip," highly visible, suave, charismatic, and full of celebrity star-power. (He was like Steve Wynn has been in

Vegas for many years, only Lefty was a lot more visible than Wynn. Of course, visibility was a lot easier then. The casinos were the size of some of the Hollywood living rooms I used to frequent.)

Lefty started hanging around the Dunes in between shows so he could keep an eye on his prized possession. Then Geri and Lefty would vanish after the second show, while the rest of us mixed.

Finally, five years after her transformation to a Vegas show-girl, Geri and Frank Rosenthal were married and continued to be the darlings of the social scene on the Strip. They were seen everywhere, and all the girls were glad that Geri seemed to have it all. But we didn't know that she really had...too much. Too much of alcohol and drugs, and too much of Tony "The Ant" Spilotro. That man made my skin crawl whenever I'd see him. He looked like a rat—a short, cocky, wife-cheater rat. He was not a nice guy. But, Geri had been seeing him before Lefty and couldn't seem to shake off The Ant even after she married the King of the Strip.

The last time I saw Geri was when I had my night and day confused. One night after mixing, I was worn out. I had laughed too much, hadn't had nearly enough to drink, and had lost my "gifted" gambling money. I went home really early for me, which was about 2:30 a.m. I took a sleeping pill, fell into bed, and was gone.

When I woke up, the clock read 6:00! No! I was going to be late! I'm supposed to be on stage in an hour! I threw on some makeup and ran out of the house. Damn. I don't even have enough gas to get there! I pulled into a station and saw Geri Marmor in a big red and white Cadillac. She looked really rough. Her left ear was bandaged like a Doberman Pincer when their ears are getting trained. I asked her what happened, and she said she was in a car accident and her ear went through the driver side window. I told her she was full of shit and she just smiled. I told her she had a good life and she needed to appreciate it and stay away from Spilotro because it could only come to a bad end. She let me know just where I could stick my opinion. That was the last time I saw her.

Geri died at the age of 46 in 1981, a year after divorcing Lefty. Given her love of living in the fast lane, which included too many drugs and too many men, 46 was probably a long time for her to live.

Hmmm…this wasn't the most pleasant memory of my showgirl-working-with-the-Mob years. Let's move on to something that will make us both smile.

Cursed to Live in Interesting Times

"You look like an owl with a hangover! Your pastie fell off, and you have a big pink 'eye' with a white glue circle around it!" That was my greeting from another showgirl as I stepped backstage after a number at the Dunes. She was laughing so hard she had to hold on to the curtain to keep her three-foot headdress from tipping her over. When I looked in the mirror, I made owl-y "hoot, hoot" sounds, and then we were both try-ing to stay upright! Who said you can't have fun on the job?

Thinking about all the great things, and sometimes strange things that happened to me make me grateful that I lived "in interesting times." I'm often asked if I regret any of the less-than-usual things I did. No way! I would regret having had the chances to "go for it" and passing on them. Yes, I hit a few bumps and ran across some snakes along the way, but so what? It was all worth it, and I'd do it again—only maybe more next time!

I've always had a challenge with my attention span. I pay good attention...just not for long. If I hadn't sampled everything that came my way, I would probably have died from boredom years ago. But I didn't pass on much! I just laid down on the buffet of good times and nibbled my way down the table.

Here are some of the goodies that kept me nibbling during the Vegas times. Come along and enjoy them with me!

⌘　⌘　⌘

Something our audience didn't realize was that we could see and hear them during the show.

Some of what we heard would not have made their mothers proud! One night a group of sailors was sitting near the passerelle, the plexi-glass-covered bridge that went out into the audience and curved across the front of the stage. As we pranced past them, we could hear their mouths running. "That's a guy. That's not a chick. He must be a fag dressing up like that. I'd like to show him what sailors do to fags!" Yeah, yeah, yeah...you're macho. We're impressed.

We had Jill Kreiger in our line at the time—a tall redhead who really should have been a comedian. She could change and throw her voice to mimic different women or men, and she had a super-quick, super-funny mind. As we came across the passerelle again, the sailors started mouthing off again.

"Trying to pass those fags off like they're girls! They're not even men! We can show the fags real men."

Jill's John Wayne voice boomed out, "You're right, and I'd really like to suck your dick after the show." The sailors hollered in shock (actually, it sounded like sissy-girl screams to us), and they were scrambling to get as far from the passerelle as possible. They really wanted to jump ship! People all around them were repeating Jill's "request," and it was moving around the showroom like the Telephone Game. "I'd really like to suck your dick," over and over.

That broke up the whole showgirl line. We were laughing out loud, headdresses were tipping, and tits were jiggling. We had to hold on to each other to get off stage! (I'm laughing right now, seeing again the shock on the sailors' faces. Thanks U.S. Navy; I needed that!)

After the show, there they were waiting for us with their cute little Dixie Cup sailor hats in their hands, and their eyes down. "Ma'am, we're really sorry about the way we behaved in the show. That just wasn't right. We know you're girls because..." At this point, the sailor spokesman realized he was going into dangerous territory and didn't know how to pull himself to safety, so his apology just trailed off. We told them, "No harm, no foul, guys." We let them hang out with us the rest of the night, buying us drinks and getting their pictures taken with a whole bevy of lovelies. I wonder how they told this story when they got back to their ship.

⌘　⌘　⌘

I remember another night when we exacted revenge—showgirl style—when people couldn't seem to just watch and enjoy, but thought they were showgirl critics too. It was at the Dunes, performing in Casino de Paris, and we were wearing some of the biggest and heaviest costumes I ever carried around. Entire ostriches had to have been stripped bald to make each of those skirts and headpieces.

During the show, we would go running and screaming around the passerelle several times. (Try doing that when you're covered with feathers!) Two couples were sitting right next to the bridge, and we could hear the women's unappreciated comments. "She has terrible tits." "She's too fat to be a showgirl." "My ugly niece could do better than that." "Where'd they get her—Woolworths?" "Those boy dancers are all fags." A few runs around the passerelle and a few more comments and we all had a huge hate-on going for those people!

When it was time to crown Napoleon in the show, we had to put on almost floor-length, close to 30-pound, fur and velvet capes. Actually, we didn't put them on. We stepped backstage where it took two dressers to lay each cape on us. Then they'd give us a little shove to help jump-start our walking down the passerelle again. As we passed those mangy couples, we started flipping our capes, sweeping them over their ugly heads. One guy's glasses went flying, both women lost their wigs, and they all lost their drinks. So good. Sometimes a girl's just gotta' have fun.

That passerelle put us more up-front and personal with our audience, but it sure caused us some grief too. I don't know why people figured that was a good place to put their drinks when they had already seen us sweeping down that bridge! (*I hope you never did that when you were in Vegas. Did you? Shake your head, "No."*)

⌘   ⌘   ⌘

One night at the Trop, wearing a huge hooped skirt, I was holding my spot on the passerelle, inches away from the audience. They were staring only at me, smiling and laughing. "Gee, I must really look cute tonight," I thought "Look at all the attention I'm getting." I finally felt something on my thigh. One of the men had crept up under my skirt, and his hand was grabbing my thigh! I kicked at him, he released his grip on my leg, and he lost a tooth. I got in a little trouble over that deal. But don't be putting your ugly-ass hands on me!

⌘   ⌘   ⌘

Same hoop skirt, same show at the Trop, but a different night. I was standing right behind the main curtain waiting for it to go up so that we could take our second bow. There was one problem though—I wasn't far enough behind the curtain. I was filling in for some girl who just hadn't shown up that night, so I wasn't exactly sure where I was supposed to be. As the curtain began to rise, my metal hoop got caught and started to lift, higher, higher, higher. The audience was roaring while I was worried about my life! I worked feverishly to get the one hook holding that huge skirt on me unlatched, but it didn't break loose until the hoop was over my head. Whew! I was freed from the curtain-trapped skirt, and it could continue to rise in the air without me attached. Then the audience really went wild! There I was, standing with just my mesh tights attached to my G-string with safety pins. And that night, I had worn my favorite G-string with the little ducks print! Oh, the humiliation!

The "cursed" hoop dress!

⌘ ⌘ ⌘

The rude women who had their wigs whipped off at the Dunes were right when they said the boy dancers were fags. But we didn't usually call them that, although we could have if we wanted to. They were our friends and our drinking, motorcycling, water-skiing buddies. We didn't say *gay* either.

We just weren't too PC then. Hell, we didn't even know what *politically correct* meant.

The other "gay" type was a little harder to spot from the audience. For reasons I've never figured out, the showgirl life style and particular shows seemed to attract a lot of lesbians. The Dunes show, in particular, seemed to be a lesbian magnet. That wasn't usually a problem for us. If we didn't swing that way, we all knew how to say, "No." They could do whatever they wanted with each other. Until, they started doing it a lot with each other at the Dunes!

Every night, you were stumbling across two (or more) of them doing what they do. *Okay, I'll pause for a minute while you think about that. Let me know when you're done.* They were on the roof, in the dressing rooms, and in the shower. We got a little tired of stepping over or around the lovers-in-action.

One day, Major Riddle showed up in the dressing room. Although he was the genius behind bringing Minsky's Follies to Vegas, and it was well known that he had a real interest in show-girls, as the owner of the Dunes he didn't usually come down to the dressing rooms. But there he was, and he was not happy.

"I know that half of you are queer. I don't know which half, so I'm going to fire every other one." He counted each of us and all the odd numbered girls were fired. (I was glad I was number six that night!) It might not have been fair, but it did cut down on the moaning in the showers—not all the way though.

Major Riddle's "bet" that he'd pick the right girls with the odd/even method was as good as his poker bets. He was the biggest fish in Vegas—lots of money, but no skill and no luck at the tables. But he just wouldn't stop playing. Riddle went from seven-eighths ownership of the Dunes to one-eighth in one year in the high-stakes games at the Aladdin—just pissed it away with no-limit Texas Hold 'Em.

⌘ ⌘ ⌘

We made the same moves and hit the same marks to stand in every show that it got to be instinctive. Our minds would just zone out, and we'd distract ourselves with other things, like "What do I need from the grocery store," or, "If that ass-hole doesn't call tonight, I'm done with him," or, "What was that guy on Table 4 thinking with that ugly witch with him? Doesn't he know you get a dog for $20 in Vegas?"

One night, just to have something to think about, I decided to count the number of stairs I had to go up and down in the Folies show. My first appearance was to descend from the ceiling on a rickety plywood platform, throw my hand in the air, and announce, "Ladies and Gentleman, the Riviera proudly presents the Folies Bergere." Then I'd go back up, jump off the platform, and join the rest of the girls for our run down the long staircase onto the stage.

I counted every stair through the first show. Then I counted them through the second show. I wanted to remember my count for the third show that night, so I kept repeating "eleven hundred and thirty-two" during the quick turn-around before the last show. As I descended from the ceiling, I said dramatically, "Ladies and Gentlemen, eleven hundred and thirty-two!" The audience stared at me and I stared back. What was that? Did that come out of my mouth? Oh well, smile and pretend like it didn't happen. Just finish the rest of the line and get back up into the ceiling.

As I ran backstage, the boss said, "What the hell was that?" I gave him the what-are-you-talking-about look and took my position. I would never acknowledge what I had said, and soon enough, everyone else thought they were the crazy ones. (I finished the count in the third show. There were 1,698 stairs to climb in all three shows. And I wondered why my calves hurt! *Have you ever wondered why show-girls have such great looking legs? There it is…1,698 stairs. Do not try that at home.*)

⌘ ⌘ ⌘

Remembering that rickety plywood platform reminds me of the time I almost turned into a Flying Wallenda about 20 feet above the audience!

There were actually four of us who came down from the ceiling on those platforms to announce the beginning of each Folies show. Two of the others who were regulars on the platforms were Felicia Atkins and Joyce Grayson. They were both gorgeous, in-demand showgirls who deserved the long runs in Vegas that they both enjoyed. (Actually Felicia's long run should have been longer. The hotels, well after the Mob era, started making everyone audition about every 18 months for each new show. Although Felicia had been a principal show-girl for 20 years, she had to audition along with the just-showed-up-in-Vegas wanna-bes. Someone must have thought that Felicia's time was done, so they just didn't pick her up after her audition. They didn't have even the courtesy to retire her gracefully. Bastards.)

The Folies platform that tried to kill me!

We'd walk up too many stairs to get above the ceiling, get our mikes on, and climb down onto the open-sided piece of wood. There was a small bar across the back and a wire on each corner connected to the up and down gears. Once the orchestra started playing, the gears would begin to turn, and we'd appear high above the audience's heads. We'd say our announcing lines and then slowly go back up, jump off the platform, remove the mikes, and hurry over to the staircase to join the rest of the girls. At least that's how it worked most of the time.

One night, I had a premonition and asked the stage hand what would happen if the platform fell. He said, "Oh, don't worry about it. If it falls, all four of you will go down." I don't know why he thought that was comforting. Maybe I'd feel better figuring I wouldn't die alone? Not.

A few nights later, as we were coming out of the ceiling, I heard too much grinding, and the platform started jerking and banging against the back wall. This was so not good. I leaned against the bar and grabbed one of the wires behind me. I'm thinking, "Should I holler to the other girls to warn them? He said we'd all fall! But what if nothing happens? Then I'll sound like Chicken Little."

Before I could decide whether I should warn the others that "the sky was falling," one of the front wires snapped off the pulley, whipped past me, and then just hung there. My platform tipped, and I was hanging on to the bar with one hand and looking down over the people, who looked like little Munchkins from that height. My instant reaction was to find somebody down there who could break my fall. Holy shit!

A stagehand started yelling, "Get the wire! Hold on to it!" I reached out and begin flipping my arm, winding the wire tighter and tighter to keep me connected to it! All the stage-hands started lifting the platform up by hand, and I got off just as the wire broke through my shredded-to-pieces long gloves.

But the show must go on, so I raced over to the staircase and got into position—minus the destroyed glove. I made all my moves and hit all my spots in the show on auto-pilot, while I re-lived just how close that was to being my last show!

This happened in the first show that night! We were supposed to go back up there and do it again for the second show. We were all afraid of the platform, and a couple of the girls were crying. The boss came to me and said, "They have it fixed. You need to get back up there. If you go, the others will too."

Now, I loved being in the show, but not so much that I was willing to die for it! But good (financial) sense prevailed, and I figured that if I was going to do it, it had to be worth the risk.

"Okay, I'll go and I'll get them to go, but I want an extra $500 under the table." After the powers-that-be agreed, I rounded up the other girls and told them, "Get your big girl panties on. We're going to do it again." And we did, and the platform stayed up, and I went shopping the next day.

⌘ ⌘ ⌘

The costumes were not only huge and heavy and (mostly) beautiful—a few of them were dangerous too. For one of our numbers in the Folies, we had butt-ugly red outfits with a wired hoop sticking out about mid-thigh with long, snarly, white feathers hanging off the hoop. Below that was a way-too-tight long skirt. We were supposed to run down that staircase (again!) with those skirts when we could barely move our legs, wearing 3½" heels and without looking down!

One night, one girl didn't make it, and she tumbled down the stairs, landing hard at the bottom and breaking her arm. The good news was that she was still in her right spot for the showgirl line. (Well, maybe not good news for her, but it was for us.) Showgirls know the show must go on. We never broke the line. Two of the girls just moved in on each side of her and picked her up, and the entire line made a grand exit to the side stage, where we unceremoniously handed her over to a stagehand. We had "rescued" her without missing a beat.

The girl didn't return to the show after her arm healed. I think she didn't want to face that sausage skirt again.

That was the accident that I witnessed and helped hide from the audience. The one I'm sorry I missed was when Gloria Tiffany fell out of the ceiling during the second show at the Stardust. She had more than her quota of five drinks during the between-shows dinner break, and she was drop-dead drunk. And she did drop! She fell right on top of some guy. Gloria was not a lightweight. She was 5'11" and weighed about 160 pounds. She must have felt like the Great Pumpkin landing on him! The guy sued, Gloria was fired, and the whole event was the talk of the Strip until something else weird (or interesting) popped up.

⌘　⌘　⌘

One of the funniest men I ever worked with was George Gobel. He not only had them rolling in the aisles during his show, but he was even more fun backstage. He did seem to get a lot funnier the more Cutty Sark he drank, and he drank it all night every night! By the time the show was over, George was plastered and would sit on a low chair backstage nodding off, which made his eyes all squinty. Every night, he'd repeat the same "command." "Don't anybody leave. I'm watching. I know if anybody's leaving. I'm just waiting in the tall grass like a snake." We'd tell him the next night that he said it again, and he'd just laugh…and at the end of the night, there he was "waiting in the tall grass like a snake." Funny, funny man!

⌘ ⌘ ⌘

Milton Berle was another great comedian and a very kind man. I'd often go to his dressing room to look at the pictures of his family. He was particularly fond of a photo of his father and him when he was about 12 years old. Milton would tell me wonderful, loving stories of his family and his growing-up years. I thought it was so sweet that he had those pictures with him in Vegas and that he wanted to share with me.

However, Milton also had a hysterical prankster side! One of the jokes in Hollywood used to be "Who has the biggest dick in town." The answer was "Ruth Berle." (That was and probably still is, an ongoing Hollywood competition. The "biggest in town" used to be Milton Berle's distinction, with the honor passing on to Ed Bagley Jr., and then to Liam Neeson.)

One night, Milton gave a party, and he was passing around an hors d'oeuvre tray to his guests. Resting comfortably in the parsley…was his dick! Yep, he had something to brag about! *Don't even think about doing that! It's another one of those "not recommended to try this at home." But if you do…would you let me know? That's just too funny!*

⌘ ⌘ ⌘

Siegfried and Roy debuted in Vegas at the Tropicana in 1967 with a 12-minute show during the Folies. They came with two cheetahs and a bunch of flamingos for their act. We didn't have to deal with the birds, but those cheetahs were all over backstage. Either Siegfried or Roy was always walking them around on a leash with a bowl of meat, and they'd poke their heads into our dressing room. Try to get your makeup on straight when a cheetah's head pops up in your mirror! Lipstick up to your eyebrows!

One night, while we were changing to go back on after their show, we heard a ruckus out front, and we all ran to the curtains to sneak a peek. Instruments were crashing around, chairs tipping over, people hollering, and the piano music was getting louder and louder. Seems the leash on one of the cats had played out too far, and the cheetah had jumped into the orchestra pit. All the musicians were scrambling to get out of the pit, except for the piano player. I don't think he missed a note. He just kept playing with that big cheetah sitting on top of his piano staring at him. Another man who knew that the show must go on!

⌘　⌘　⌘

In 1967 (I remember that year), I was working a show at the Frontier. That was not the highlight of my showgirl career, except for one very special reason. Actually, I should write "except for one very special *person*." The Frontier had brought in a show starring Karel Gott who was billed as the Golden Voice of Prague. There was a whole entourage from Czechoslovakia with Gott, including several super-sized, good-looking Czech dancers, some ugly little acrobats, a bunch of bodyguards following them around holding on to their passports, and a very special composer/musician named Ladislav

"Ladi" Staidl. None of the Czech troupe spoke English, except for Karel and Ladi, who each had about a 50-word vocabulary.

I had taken some of the Czech troupe under my wing (mostly to be around Ladi) and would take them around to the various lounge shows. I carried a well-used Czech dictionary with me, but we still had a few communication issues.

One day, they wanted to see the jazz singer Morgana King's show. I thought it was pretty funny that the Czechs didn't know who Dean Martin was, but they all sure knew Morgana. Go figure. Six guys and my friend Gerri piled into my Buick Riviera for an afternoon on the town.

However, before we could see Morgana, we had to stop so they could buy blue jeans! They explained in a really bad English/Czech combination (while I thumbed through my dictionary) that in Communist countries, blue jeans were like gold. They bought about 50 pairs of jeans. Now the car was full and so was the trunk.

We finally got to the show and were leaving when three not-at-all-cute, 20-something girls were walking across the parking lot. The guys began chattering like crazy in Czech.

Gerri said to me, "Oh my God, they think those dogs are cool!"

"Dogs? What is dogs?" one of them asked. I pointed to the girls. There was more Czech chattering.

Later that night, I was making love to Ladi at my home, and we had made it from the couch to the bed to the floor. When we were finished, and exhausted, he said "I'm very, very happy. I have my own dog." If we hadn't already been on the floor, I would have fallen on it, laughing my "doggy" ass off!

Ladi was very, very special, and my relationship with him would cover a few years and a few more countries. (That's coming up too.)

⌘ ⌘ ⌘

One night at the Frontier, our backstage guards and some of the entertainers had gone outside for a smoke, and a little brown street dog had followed the Czech troop back inside. I saw the dog when he poked his nose into my dressing room where I was getting ready for the next show. I had on my G-string, tights, gloves, jewelry, and heels, but not much else so far. Suddenly, I heard hollering and yipping and ran out to see the security guy beating the dog with his stick! Now, I'm not an animal fanatic. When my cat Spoons goes, I'll be sad, but I won't lie down and die over it. But I am a fanatic about people being cruel to anyone or anything.

I ran out in my pre-show garb screaming, "Don't touch that dog! Leave him alone!" The security guy hit the dog again, called me a cunt, and shoved me. I went bug-fuck crazy. I went after him with my fists and anything else I could get my hands on, including a chair, his stick, and my high heels. The guy was either too shocked or too afraid to really fight back, and I beat the shit out of him. When they pulled me off, I was on top of him hammering him with my shoe. (Somebody had rescued the dog.) They fired me without notice. So what... the Frontier was a crappy show anyway. I just called up Carl and started at the Trop again a week later.

Even though I hated the Frontier show, firing me like that without notice for rescuing a cute little dog just totally pissed me off. This is what I wrote in my diary that night.

Now, **that's** a headdress!

Fired at the Frontier without notice. I am putting an enormous pox on the following:

Alan Lee, Fred Hattel, Jack Shapiro, Bill Lundy
No wish is too evil for them. I wish I were a witch so I could turn them into frogs or pigs or something. Of course, only because of their shapes are they mistaken for humans now.

The Frontier and my short rebound gig at the Trop were my last shows in Vegas. I was a showgirl just one more time after that when I appeared in the Femmes de Paris in 1968, in Anaheim. It was some kind of strange karma that the producers of my last show were the same two guys who produced my first show; Danny Dare and Sammy Lewis. I had come full circle in my showgirl life.

I knew that my time as a showgirl had come to an end. Why? I was only 31. I recently looked at a promo shot advertising the Femmes de Paris, and I was still seriously hot! But I had lost my edge. I still had the heart of a showgirl, but I had lost the drive and the need to do it again. It was getting harder for me to hear the applause.

A special thing that happened at the Frontier helped me lose that drive to hear the applause no matter what it took. No, it wasn't beating the crap out of the guard. That special thing was that I fell in love with Ladi Staidl and spent the next several years in a multi-country quest to straighten out my married life (yes, I was married then), my love life, my professional life, and my head.

Come with me to Hollywood, and I'll fill in the blanks for you.

Four

Made in Hollywood

Growing up Hollywood

"You must have screwed everyone in Hollywood! I was at a party last night, and every guy there was saying, 'Oh, you must be Lisa's sister.'" My sister Karen was giving me a hard time one day at lunch. Karen, Karen, Karen...how many times do I have to tell you? No, I don't do celebrities.

I have never been a star-fucker. All I can hear when I'm around them is, "Gimme, gimme, take me, buy me, do me." It's not that they're easy; most stars go way beyond easy. They figure as soon as you get close enough to catch a whiff of their cologne-soaked bodies, you're supposed to assume the missionary position. Why do some girls do that? Inside tip: For guys who are so proud of their dicks, stars sure don't treat them right. They'll stick those things just about anywhere. Now, isn't that a scary thought? Doesn't make me want to get horizontal! Besides that, they all look like their glossies when they get that rolling-eyed "do me" look. Call me old-fashioned, but I think you should probably care about a person (and not just one of their "parts") before you play Romper Room.

Well...maybe I did play Romper Room just a little. But damn, some things were just too good to pass up! I wanted to change my name to Jane for a few months when I was dating Ron Ely, who was Tarzan on TV, for several seasons. Trust me when I tell you—he was **Tarzan**! Swinging through trees, fighting off lions, just walking around Hollywood, and in bed—Tarzan! Unfortunately, being with Ron was a problem. Every time we went out, somebody wanted to take on Tarzan. It was widespread knowledge that Ron didn't use a stunt double for his rope swinging and animal fighting, and every guy out there wanted to show that he could take on Tarzan. I knew we'd reached the end of our date when some drunk started in with, "Oh you think you're so tough, don't you? Well, how about showing just how tough you are? Swing on this!" Being with Ron was too much hassle—but while it lasted, oh my God!

Okay, and then there was Ken Clark, who was a rugged man's man. I'd seen him in *South Pacific* when he played Stewpot, and I remember thinking at the time—"That's what a man is supposed to look like!" It just felt right to spend a little "quality" time with Ken. Yep, I'd been thinking right. Ken not only looked the way a man should, he also knew how to use that incredible body. Unfortunately for Ken, however, he knew how to keep himself hunky, but he didn't do himself a lot of favors with some of his career choices. Starring in *Attack of the Giant Leeches* and a bunch of other B (or less) movies right after *South Pacific* didn't exactly endear Ken to Hollywood producers. Our good times ended when he decided he needed to seek his fortunes in Spaghetti Westerns in Europe.

Now, don't be badgering me to tell you more stories about my Hollywood Wild Rides. Didn't I already tell you that I wasn't a star-fucker? And I wasn't. Well, not most of the time. Okay, if I remember any more stories that I think you should know about, I'll tell you later. Maybe.

There's no way I could have grown up star-struck. Being around actors and celebrities was the natural order of things. I really did believe that Hollywood was the way everyone lived; it was "normal." One reason for my less-than-impressed attitude is that I was raised around stars, and I saw them in their ratty bathrobes in the yard. Except for having long, black limos pick them up every once in awhile, they were just the people next door.

I grew up in Los Feliz, California, which is next to Hollywood and Griffith Park. Sunset Boulevard and Hollywood Boulevard run right into Los Feliz, so that neighborhood had always been (and still is today) a real favorite with movie people. It has all the right celebrity-friendly elements. The lots are large and privacy-landscaped, it's close to everything, the houses are mini- or full mansions, and the neighbors are discrete. (They have to be. "You don't talk trash about me, and I won't tell on you.")

More recently, Madonna and Brad Pitt had (or have) homes in Los Feliz, along with others who to and fro from many neighborhoods in L.A. But when I was growing up, it was Alan Ladd, Ray Milland, Cecile B. DeMille, William Bendix, and Jack Dempsey. These were "solid" celebrities who actually lived in their houses, raised families, and hung around for awhile.

My parents weren't in the movie business, however; we just lived around the movie people. My father had a ton of money because he was part of the Malouf family that owned Mode O'Day stores, and eventually Dad was the president of the company. (*Do you remember Mode O'Day clothes? If you have any hanging around in your closet, you might want to put them on eBay. I understand they're going for some decent money.*) There were over 600 stores and six factories making most of the clothes, and Dad's company made some serious money almost up to the time it closed in 1984.

Mom and Dad bought our house in 1940 for $4,000, which covered the lien against the contractor for the lumber cost to build it. The house had East Coast elegant style with a long, wide, curving sidewalk leading up the hill to the front door. It was two stories with a tuck-under garage, huge windows, and very cool art deco lights and doors. (I have an ad for our house from months ago when it was on the market for $1.6 million. Damnation. I wish my mother had kept that house! I'd be living it in today—probably with my sisters!)

We had all the "accessories" that everyone else in our neighborhood had, like a maid (who made me help clean all the time and could never seem to wake me up on time for school.) My mother, Alice, always drove a new Cadillac, which used to embarrass me when she'd drop me off at school, so I'd make her drop me off a block away. Some of my classmates at our Catholic school were recruited from the non-Cadillac areas around Los Feliz, and I didn't want to seem like a "rich kid." Besides, what kid wants to be seen with her mother? (Some things have always been the same.)

When people (non-Californians) would find out where I'd grown up, they'd ask, "Did you get any autographs?" What? *Now, I know you're not asking this, because you probably know better, but let's think this through together. When you were growing up, did you get autographs from "Mary Anne and Joe" who lived two houses down, or that scary "Old Man Charlie" who lived at the end of your block? I'll bet you didn't. You probably just knocked on Mary Anne and Joe's door to get their kids to come out to play, and you canvassed the whole neighborhood at Halloween to get a really good sugar buzz on. That's what I did too—played with their kids in the street and filled up my paper bag with candy. You and I grew up the same, but just maybe my neighbors wore more makeup—the women and the men—and I probably got better candy.*

Now that I think about it, I do have some stand-out memories of some of our neighbors. One of them is Halloween. For several years, my sisters and I loved to go to Cecil B. DeMille's house. He lived on one of the higher hills in the neighborhood, and we had to walk up this super-long driveway and go through tall iron gates to get to the front door. But it was worth the walk. Even though all the other friends of my parents were "Uncle" and "Aunt," Mr. DeMille was "Mr. DeMille," even to my mother and dad. He was just so elegant and so well regarded in the industry and in the neighborhood. Besides, he had done *The Ten Commandments*—that alone puts a person in a God-like category.

Mr. DeMille would always be dressed in a tuxedo when he answered the doorbell himself, and he'd open the door wide for us trick-or-treaters to step just inside. That's when we'd see his beautiful wife (who we only referred to as Mrs. DeMille) sitting like a queen in a big, brocade chair. I remember one year that she had on a long, gold gown, which my kid brain thought must have been made out of real gold. The bottom of the full dress was swirled on the floor all around her in a wide circle. I realize now that Mr. DeMille must have positioned her like that for all of us to see. He was the ultimate director, setting up a great shot! Mrs. DeMille would just smile and say, very kindly, "Happy Halloween," as Mr. DeMille handed out great handfuls of candy.

Our other neighbors were just pretty normal. Well, maybe there were those who were right-on-the-edge. Alan Ladd lived near us, and he was a real sun worshipper. If the sun was out (which is pretty much all the time in California), he was in his back yard lapping up rays. Later in the day, the sun would move to the front, and so would Alan. My sisters and I would make a point to casually, and slowly, stroll by his house when we figured he'd be tanning in the front yard. He was "very interesting." Not because he was Alan Ladd (remember *Shane?*), but because he sunbathed in a black Speedo. This was the early '50s—a black Speedo was more than a little out-there! We enjoyed the view at Ladd's house, until our mother heard us talking about it and asked Alan to either stay in his back yard or cover up. Spoiler.

If he would have stayed out there just a little longer, I might have had a better understanding of male anatomy than I did as a teenager. Of course, I knew all about sex from my friends at Immaculate Heart High School, but like most of that kind of information from Catholic school girls, it was pretty flawed. All the girls were talking about it "doing it," but nobody had first-hand information, so I decided it was my responsibility to my girlfriends' continuing education to lose my virginity. The guy I picked to help me with this task was 30 years old. It was an unremarkable, no-news event, except for one thing. When he took off his pants, I got a little freaked out! I thought I'd hooked up with some hermaphrodite! (We had giggled about that at school.) I knew he couldn't be all boy because he had pubic hair! I thought it only grew on girls. Alan Ladd could have helped me out with that misunderstanding with just a slightly smaller Speedo.

My sixteenth birthday heralded my "coming out" in several categories, actually. I did a little sex and a lot of makeup, and I learned about the benefits of gambling. I would check the horse race entrants in the *Examiner* for every race day. Then

I'd get my classmates together to pick one horse for each race. They'd have to give me 50 cents, and if the horse came in first, second, or third, I'd double their money. If their horse lost, I'd keep the money, of course. Those girls were not handicappers. I made about eight bucks a week.

For awhile, our neighborhood was director-heavy, with Mr. DeMille on one side of us and "Uncle" Frank Borzage on the other. Uncle Frank was pretty old when he lived near us, but he had already won a couple of Academy Awards, including the first one ever given, for directing *Street Angel,* and another one for *Bad Girl.* He was a widower when he moved into our neighborhood and didn't remarry, but because he was still directing a lot of pictures during the '40s, Uncle Frank was always in the company of good-looking men and women who arrived in limos. He was nice to all of us kids and would stop and talk for awhile. (But he didn't give out DeMille-quality Halloween treats, so he was further down on the preferred list.)

We went by Uncle Frank's house often because he lived right next door to the Wittkins. Betty Wittkins was my ultimate, all-time role model who (unknowingly) set the pattern for my life. She was the way I thought women should be—certainly the way I wanted to be—and she led the life that I figured was my destiny. I was just mesmerized by Betty Wittkins from the first time I met her. I, of course, called her Mrs. Wittkins when I was introduced, but she said, "Oh, no dear. Not Mrs. Wittkins. You can call me Betty."

It was like she was saying to me, and me alone, "I can see that you're not just a kid. You're grown up enough to call me by my first name." Instant love. I felt completely sophisticated being on a first-name basis with a woman who was so beautiful and so worldly. I also thought it was incredible when Betty told me that her maiden name had been Hind. She grew up B. Hind! I would have been mortified with that name, but she was so cool that she thought it was funny!

Betty had been a model, and she always held on to the classic '50s look: wide hips, big boobs, and a little waist. She knew how to dress to show off that figure, too! We weren't sure what her husband Matty did, because she said vaguely that he was an "importer." We knew that he was gone a lot, but when he'd return, he had silk fabric from the Orient that she'd have made into skin-tight dresses that she wore every day.

Well, almost every day—not when she was lying around her pool in her bikini, or naked. I thought both ways of "dressing" were just so cool. A bikini was just not worn by many people then, and certainly not "mothers." (Betty had three kids who were our play-in-the-street friends.)

Betty's life was how it was supposed to be. When her husband (Mr. Wittkins, to us) came home, she would be fussing over him and catering to him all the time—up to and including bleaching the hair on his chest at the pool. (If I hadn't thought Betty was so wonderful, I would have been grossed out.) The fact that Mr. Wittkins was often gone really appealed to me too. Because it was Betty's life that I really wanted for my own, I decided that's the way it was supposed to be. Husbands were supposed to take lots of extended business trips, come home with gifts, get pampered, and leave again. I thought my family was completely weird because my father came home every night and we had dinner together at six o'clock. Ugghh...

And when Mr. Wittkins was away, Betty was at the pool with her friends, looking elegant and sipping champagne out of real crystal flutes. She even used glass at the pool! She broke so many rules that I'd grown up with—I loved it! (I'll bet she even ran with scissors—looking hot while she did it! And if I had seen her do that, I would have done it too.)

I wanted to look like, be like, and live like Betty, and many of the zigs and zags I made in my life were because I was "seeking Betty." With Betty as my muse, is it a surprise that I took the road that led to my model, actress, showgirl, independent, fun-loving Wild Rides?

Betty had two boys, Bernard and Matthew, and a daughter named Regina, and several times a week we all gathered together. One day, when I was 12 years old, my sister Barbara and I were going up the dirt path (our shortcut) to Betty's house to get our friends, when my mother came streaking down the driveway screaming at us to come home right away. How embarrassing was that? We turned right around just so the rest of the neighborhood wouldn't see our forever-pregnant mother chasing after us! We didn't know for quite awhile why we were called back or why our mother was talking hush-hush on the phone all afternoon or why there were so many cars driving up and down our usually quiet street. Here's why...

Betty had a friend named Sylvia Hausman who had two kids who she'd bring over to Betty's so that we could all play together. A couple of times, Sylvia's father would even come with them and bring us neat things to play with. I remember the Nik L Nips that were five small wax bottles in a little carton. Each bottle had a different flavor of really gross syrup. We'd chew the whole thing, wax and all. Our favorite toy that Sylvia's father brought us was the elastic, smelly bubbles that came in a tube that we'd blow up with a straw. After we'd break the bubbles, we'd chew the plastic. (That stuff tasted so bad, it had to be toxic. But that didn't stop us. I'm pretty sure that crap had to have killed a lot of kids' brain cells though.)

The excitement on our street that day in November of 1949 was that Sylvia was trying to recover at the Wittkins house after the arrest of her father, Fred Stroble, who lived with them in Culver City. Fred had been arrested three days after raping and killing Linda Glucoft, a six-year-old girl who was Sylvia's daughter, Rochelle's friend. After little Linda (and Stroble) had not shown up the night of the murder, the police searched until they found her body the next day. She was wearing only her yellow socks and red shoes, and she was wrapped in an Indian blanket, covered with trash, and wedged behind an incinerator—in the Hausmans' backyard! The murder weapons—a bloodstained ax, hammer, ice pick, and butcher knife—were lying there beside her.

Stroble had been previously arrested for exposing himself to a 10-year-old, but he hadn't shown up for his court date, and the cops hadn't gone after him. There was one more child molester on the loose! The Hausmans, who had joined in the search, got suspicious because Fred was gone too and told the police about his record. A truck driver recognized Fred from pictures that were being distributed and called in a tip, and Stroble was found in a bar, just hanging out and having a beer. He went away quietly in handcuffs. In his confession he said, "I had to kill her to stop her screaming. I wanted to play with her and she refused. This wasn't the first time. I had played with her once before." Stroble also admitted to police that he had molested several other children around Los Angeles over a number of years.

This was the Fred Stroble who brought us Nik L Nips and elastic bubbles! No wonder my mother was so upset! A few good things came out of this nightmare, however. As a result of Stroble's arrest in the state of California, molesting a child became a felony, and the sex killing of a child under 14 became punishable by the death penalty or life in prison without parole. Fred Stroble was executed...another good thing that came out of the situation. Another pervert was off the streets.

Los Angeles has since put the ax that Stroble used to kill Linda Glucoft in the Los Angeles Police Department Museum. What the hell are they thinking?! Nobody should go to see that thing! *Promise me right now that you won't go to see it. That's monster shit.*

Well, that story was just too depressing, wasn't it! Okay... let's move on out of my neighborhood and into my school— another reason why I thought growing up Hollywood was normal. My Catholic high school, my classmates, and the religion that I was spoon-fed daily are contributors to how Lisa Medford turned out to be...whatever she is today.

Religion in My Oatmeal

"This doesn't make sense to me. You said that eating meat on a Friday was a mortal sin. And so is French kissing. And so is murdering anybody. So, if I don't go to confession, I'm going to go to hell for eating a hamburger and kissing and killing my mother? I'm going to go to the same hell? This just doesn't sound fair."

I was just trying to explain my morality confusion, but I got the same answer that I heard a lot from Sister Margaret at Immaculate Heart: "Loretta, go to the hall and stand there."

There was a lot about religion that didn't make sense to me—there still is. I sure had large enough doses of it to know what I didn't know. My father was Greek Orthodox, and my mother was Roman Catholic. I started out being baptized and dragged to the Greek Orthodox church because wives always followed their husband's lead back then. But my mother was concerned because my father's church-going was a little spotty, so when I was six, I was baptized in the "regular" Catholic church, and now I had to go to confession every Saturday, Mass every Sunday, and to both churches on the big holidays! And I had to go to Catholic school for my whole life, **and** I was supposed to say the Rosary every night with my mother! I really suspect that religion was spooned into my oatmeal every morning. Everywhere I looked—there it was. Enough already!

I never really had a problem with anyone else being religious. If that's what turns somebody's crank, then go for it. I never tried to stop anybody from praying to…whatever god they thought might be listening. I just didn't really appreciate (or learn from) it being ladled into me!

At Immaculate Heart, I had to write a 1000-word essay on "If I were not a Roman Catholic, what would I be?" I reasoned it out. If there is one God, and if the Jews had him first, and if Jesus hadn't even been invented before the Jews had God, then Jesus must be a Jew. So, if I wasn't a Catholic, then I should be a Jew, like Jesus. In fact, with that reasoning, I should be a Jew anyway. I got an F on that paper. I don't think I ever got a passing grade in Religion, actually. I think they just "passed me along" to get me out of high school.

I may not have been (may not be) religious, but I was and am moral. I knew (know) all the Ten Commandments, and there are several (okay, a few) that I've never broken. I've definitely never messed with number five: Thou Shalt Not Kill. I figure that one gets you the express ticket to hell.

I got most of my "religion" after I graduated from high school. I got Hollywood and prayed to the gods of Technicolor who lived in my heaven, which was also called Paramount Studios. Seemed to work for me.

Even if I hadn't gotten turned off about religion at home, Immaculate Heart would have taken care of that. I hear *Catholic*, and I immediately picture the dark blue, ugly, below-the-knees uniform I wore every damn day of my teenage years! I remember ironing those scratchy white collars and the hokey cuffs that clipped on the sleeves. (Our maid refused to iron them. She was no fool. Those suckers were too hard to get flat.) We had to wear slips and black and white saddle shoes that made our feet look like canoes. Jewelry was off limits and for sure, no patent leather shoes **ever!** *You know why, don't you? I know that some of you grew up hearing that lie about boys looking up your skirt if you had on patent leather shoes. Like what were they going to see? Baggy white underpants? Victoria's Secret, they were not! You guys reading this—did you EVER see up a girl's skirt by looking at her shoes? If you did, please let me know...I want to meet the guy with the X-ray vision and the great imagination!*

The only tolerable part of our standard Catholic school-girl uniform was the blue blazer with the Immaculate Heart patch on it. Unfortunately, in the balmy California weather, we didn't get to wear that too often. And certainly, even with our down-to-there uniforms, we could never cross our legs at school, because that was masturbation. Those nuns actually said *masturbation*, like we even knew what they were talking about when we were 13 years old! So, I hear *Catholic*, and I think "dumpy clothes, standing in the hall counting tiles, and the girls who wouldn't let me into their cliques."

I was definitely not in the "in-crowd in school. I was barely on the sidewalk with my really large Lebanese nose pressed on the window looking in at them. I ran with the nerds...not the smart ones...just the nerds who were not pretty, not talented, and not considered too smart by the nuns.

I always thought I was smart, but the nuns did not share my opinion. I remember a history class when we were supposed to read 10 pages about the Aegean Sea. Okay, so I read them, looked up, and saw that everybody else was still reading. So I read the pages again and looked up again.

"Loretta Malouf, why aren't you reading?" asked the sister.

"Because I finished it," I said.

"That's impossible. You're the stupidest girl in the class. Don't tell me you already read it." Yeah, thanks for that Sister Margaret. That helped me build my self-esteem.

Okay, I had three strikes against me in school—I was definitely not pretty, the nuns thought I was stupid, and I had a rebellious streak in a school that gave no prizes for "independent thinking." I wasn't even as much of a trouble maker as the other girls made me out to be. They were always getting me in trouble for something! At least 73 percent of the time, I was the innocent bystander.

Maureen Reagan (Ronald Reagan and Jane Wyman's daughter) and I used to pal around together even though she was in the grade behind me. I wasn't happy with her for awhile when she tried to throw an egg at me and hit a nun instead. The nun knew perfectly well who had thrown the egg because she saw us, but I got blamed for it. Big deal that Maureen's dad was a hot-shot movie actor—I knew lots of hot-shot movie actors—they were my neighbors. That nun shouldn't have blamed me because Maureen's dad was Ronald Reagan! (After I graduated, I never saw Maureen again except on TV, but when we were Immaculate Heart friends, she was a really funny and bright girl.)

I went to school with lots of soon-to-be famous girls and daughters of celebrities—and most of them wouldn't remember Loretta Malouf today even if they still have all their supposedly-smarter-than-me wits about them. John Wayne's daughter, Linda Hope (Bob Hope's adopted daughter), Jack Dempsey's girls, Carmen Dragon (the daughter of the conductor and composer by the same name—Carmen), the Diebell girls, Kathryn (Frankie Avalon's gorgeous future wife) and Gretchen (who married John Wayne's son, Michael), and Mary Tyler Moore—none of them knew (know) who Loretta Malouf was.

Maybe Mary Tyler Moore would remember. She was the nicest of the "in" crowd and was one of the top leaders of the pack. She was in my homeroom for four years and was in all our school plays. (She was a great actress even as a teenager!) I tried out for a part in one of the plays, and even though my mother had dragged me to lots of tap and ballet classes, I didn't get the part. Mary Tyler Moore was really nice about it and stopped by my desk to say she was sorry that I wouldn't be in the play with her. Did that mean a lot to me? I still remember it 55 years later.

(Years later, I was lying in bed watching *Richard Diamond* on TV with my then-lover, Cary Grant. I was able to tell Cary something even he didn't realize about that show. My former classmate at Immaculate Heart (the nicest one) was in *Richard Diamond*. Well not all of her. The voice and the legs that opened the show belonged to Mary Tyler Moore, but the rest of her was never shown. When I told Cary that those legs were my schoolmate's, being the gentleman that he was, he said, "I wonder if she realizes that her old classmate's legs are more beautiful." Nice.)

When I'd get in trouble on my own, or when one of those snotty girls would lie about me, those nuns would torture me with grilling and grilling and grilling, just like they do on the cop shows! My parents couldn't understand why I was getting more ornery and more rebellious every year. I know why. Who's surprised that in my neighborhood, with all those movie people, with religion being force-fed to me, and with those too-cool-for-words classmates, that I did not end up with six kids making dinner every night for my not-too-faithful, boring husband? Vegas showgirl, Hollywood darling—that's what I was raised to be!

Besides, I didn't need those other girls. I had the best friend in the world—Gerri Nelson. She was with me from the second grade until the end of her "forever." And I had my sisters.

"Five Easy Pieces"

"Boy, you Malouf girls have it made! Five of you—and each one of you girls is gorgeous and funny! Everyone wants to party with the Malouf sisters—that must be great!"

Some guy at a party shared this revelation with me. I agreed. "Yeah, we're so famous in Hollywood that they even made a movie about us—*Five Easy Pieces*."

My sister Karen was mortified when she found out I said that! (She's probably going to be mad again when she reads this. *Sorry, Karen...I just had to. I still think it's funny.*)

Our neighborhood, my school, and my religion (or lack of) all contributed to the making of who I eventually became: Lisa Medford. And so did my four sisters, Barbara, Karen, Joanna, and Janice. I remember looking out my bedroom window not long after we moved to Los Feliz, watching my parents drive up to bring Barbara home from the hospital. Like lots of "first of many," I wasn't too thrilled to see that little thing show up. For three years, it had been all about Loretta, and I liked it that way. It was good that I got over that though, because my parents just kept driving up and unloading new babies every few years. Catholic, remember? If you didn't have more than three kids, the priest was likely to call you in for an emergency confession.

All five of us were the same in some ways, and very different in others. It's the "same" that kept us close all our lives and the "different" that made our lives interesting.

Barbara, the first sister who rocked my only-child world is three and a half years younger by her birth date, but she has always been five years older in level-headed, well-organized, well-planned-for living. Of all the Malouf sisters, Barbara has always been her own person. She thought things out (I'm sure she had a Plan A for her life) and had a series of interesting and successful careers without appearing in rhinestones and feathers—imagine that! (She would have made a killer showgirl though—she looked like Cleopatra.)

During one period of our lives, Barbara leased the famous On the Waterfront Café in Venice Beach from our sister, Joanna, and baby sister Janice and I joined her in the Venice

Beach venture. (Joanna owned the property then and still does today. Smart Joanna!) Barbara ran the café, I ran the bar just down from it on the boardwalk, and Janice had the hot dog concession out front. I don't remember making a ton of money, but I do remember lots of sister-laughing.

Barbara, now Barbara Joseph-Hill, did very cool business things, but her best "productions" were her beautiful daughters, Shana and Gina Joseph. Hey, I just remembered! Gina is married to James de Givenchy who is the creative director for Sotheby's Diamonds. *Hey Gina, remember your Aunt Lisa, the one who always loved you best? I could use one of those trinkets that your husband makes for Sotheby's. I'll be waiting here by the door for the FedEx driver.)*

Karen showed up four years after Barbara, and it seemed like right out of the cradle she was trying to make Barbara and me "act right." Karen was the prissiest little girl I ever met! Thank God she got over that. *You did get over it, didn't you, Karen? You're not going to be ragging on me again for that* Five Easy Pieces *crack, right?*

Karen was (and still is, as Karen Callan Cohen) wonderfully artistic with a great head for business. Growing up, she was a model, an actress, and a designer for Playboy enterprises. Her costume jewelry designs for the TV shows *Dynasty* and *Scruples* sure helped build her reputation as a top accessories creator. It didn't hurt her design business to be featured on Oprah's "O" list, either—endorsements just don't come much better than that!

Karen didn't only work designing "things;" she did the same thing with people in Hollywood. In 1978, Karen was talking with producer Blake Edwards at a party when he told her that he was thrashing around trying to find the perfect lead for the movie *10*. He had found "9s" and "9½s," but he couldn't get that elusive 10. Karen remembered Bo Derek, whom she'd met five years earlier at a party at Hugh Hefner's, and brought her to Blake's office. Blake could see immediately that Bo was the 10. Without even a screen test, Karen got Bo $35,000 for the movie, options for three more pictures, and even equal billing with co-stars Julie Andrews and Dudley Moore. Great, right? Only problem is, Bo Derek went around Karen and signed directly with Edwards, screwing Karen out of her 10 percent agent's percentage. The fight between Karen and Bo (actually between Karen and Bo's asshole husband, John Derek) was played out publically and even had a large write-up in *People* magazine in February of 1980.

Karen didn't care about the money from the suit as much as the principle of the thing—part of that early prissiness that translated to integrity later on. Karen was also designing expensive, gorgeous hair-combs during that time, which were in high demand from stars like Cher and stores like Neiman-Marcus. Besides, she was married to Michael Callan, who was a good-looking actor who'd played Jane Fonda's boyfriend in *Cat Ballou*. Karen didn't need John Derek's stupid money. (Good thing, because she didn't get it. It seems that she didn't have a $20 license to be a business manager, so she lost her suit.)

Joanna arrived just two years after Karen. I don't know why it only took two more years for her to appear. Maybe my parents thought that they'd done pretty well with Karen and were eager to try again. Or maybe they were wondering if a boy might eventually show up. Whatever the reason was, along came Joanna (Joey). Joey was born in 1947, just in time to be a real "flower child" in the '60s. With her long, dark brown hair that was perfectly straight (how did that happen?), her gorgeous legs, and her great body, she looked like Cher. That worked out well when Joey met Cher when she was 19 years old and they became life-long friends. It looked like two "Chers" hanging out together when Joey went all over the world with Sonny and Cher on their tours.

Joey's knock-out looks have always served her well, but there was one occasion when her name worked against her— her real name, Joanna. Joanna and a friend were walking along the beach in Malibu when they noticed that Johnny Carson was out on his deck. Since Joanna's friend knew Johnny, they both stopped to exchange some chit-chat, which ended when Joanna's friend said, "Hey, Johnny, let me introduce you to my friend, Joanna."

"Fuck no," Carson replied. "I don't want to meet any more Joannas! Sorry, honey." With that said, he turned right around and went back into his house.

Joey's artistic talents started early (she created the first rhinestone t-shirts) and just kept getting better—all the way up to more current times, sculpting major pieces and designing the Los Angeles, City of Angels Award.

Joey married Loren Judd, but that wasn't a "forever" union. Her second husband was Walter Staudinger, a successful and wonderfully wealthy real estate developer. With all her other designing, Joey's best "products" were two gorgeous and talented children, Sarah and Brandon. (Cher is Sarah's godmother.)

The last Malouf girl was Janice (Janis). Like the rest of the Malouf girls, Janice was drawn to arty things. She was in the right spot to indulge her artistry when she was married to David Larkham, who was the art director for Elton John's albums. Using the back of one of her old Levi's jackets, Janice embroidered the title of the *Madman Across the Water* album over a two-week period. Her husband David photographed her work to use on the cover. Janice gave her original work to Elton John. (Elton had grown to expect great gifts made by Janice. She once completely covered an umbrella stand with silver, pink, and black rhinestones when she and Elton had decided that his front entry needed a little more sizzle.)

When I was reminiscing about Janice to decide what to share with you, I found out that on Wikipedia someone else was trying to take credit for that *Madman Across the Water* cover! That totally pissed me off that her artistic contribution was being claimed by someone else. I contacted Janice's son Tavis, who put up the truth on Wikipedia that his dad, David, supplied for him. I'm sure glad that got set straight! It felt good that David, and my wonderful nephew Tavis, and I could all join up to make sure Janice got the proper recognition for her work. Unfortunately, Janice can't do it herself because she died in 2003 after a long-time fight with multiple kinds of cancer. Bummer...I'll always miss Janice.

With all five of the Malouf sisters combined, we had 12 husbands, but only one of us is currently married. We all did the "marrying" gig pretty well, just not for real long.

Someone asked our father once if he was sorry to see all of his girls get married.

"Sorry? What difference does it make? I don't have time to even miss them. Pretty soon, they get un-married and they come right back!"

Yep, that was true. But in between the marrying and not and the to-ing and fro-ing, we've had a great sister ride!

The Sixth Malouf Sister

Gerri Nelson

"A topless lobster? You think I should go to Reno and be a topless lobster showgirl? Are you fuckin' nuts? This reminds me of third grade when I played the goldfish in our school play! Remember that ugly costume?" Gerri couldn't believe that I was really suggesting that she should try out for the lobster part.

"It's not the same thing as third grade, Gerri. Hell, you're moving up the food chain. This time, you get to be a crustacean!" She glared at my response, but she went to Reno anyway and wore that really funny-looking costume! Why not? The money was great and she didn't have anything else to do right then. Besides, since the day I met her in the second grade, Gerri was the sixth Malouf sister, and she was always up for whatever craziness I could think up!

I was a grade ahead of Gerri, and I was tall and skinny. Gerri was short and fat, but that didn't matter—we were sisters then and forever. She lived in my area in Los Feliz when her dad was an LAPD police captain, like his dad had been before him.

It was always "Gerri and Loretta" in school and then "Gerri and Lisa" in Hollywood and Europe and everywhere else I lived and went, because Gerri was with me for all of those amazing times. She was a model and an actress (who had been the stunt double for Jane Fonda), she helped me get out of my crappy marriage to Mike Mancuso (stay tuned), she was a knock-out topless lobster, she was hysterically funny, and she was game for anything. She was with me for her whole life, and I was with her when she died at 54 from a lung disease. (That was pretty inevitable. She started out with one foot in the grave. Gerri had six siblings who'd died from SIDS, and she had pneumonia about 12 times when she was growing up. Smoking 3–4 packs of cigarettes a day and being anorexic her whole life didn't help overcome those problems. But Gerri did live life on her terms, and she certainly made the most of it!)

I remember a road trip we took to…somewhere. I don't remember the destination, just the journey. I was selecting and laying all my stuff out on the bed, getting ready to pack up my Louis Vuitton suitcase. I went to my nightstand to pull out the Smith and Wesson .38 Police Special that I always had with me to add to my packing pile.

"My, my, my," Gerri said. "Has it gotten so bad that you have to wound them before you fuck them?" That was so Gerri!

She made me laugh so hard I almost forgot my douche bag and had to run into the shower to retrieve it and throw it on top of the suitcase. Okay, ready. We packed our suitcases in the back of my Corvette, and we were on the road, driving through the desert to…(it still hasn't come to me)… at about 60 mph.

An armored car passed me—passed my Corvette with an armored car! Wow! They were getting pretty frisky with their cargo! They waved and we smiled and waved back, and then passed them. This happened again. The armored car went around us, with the two guys grinning bigger this time, and we waved back and gave them a little wink. (They were obviously willing to risk their lives driving at that speed in that vehicle, so we figured they needed something for a reward.)

Then, there they came again—passing us for the third time. This time, one of the guys was holding up a money bag like a come-on! Gerri immediately reached back, grabbed my douche back that was sitting on top of my suitcase, and as we roared past them, she held the douche bag "high and proud." That armored car damn near ran off the road! We laughed for years over the looks on those guys' faces!

Even though I never really knew where I was going (and still don't)...I've always been really clear about where I came from. My huge Lebanese, religious, slightly-privileged family along with the try-to-break-my-spirit-while-pursuing-the-futility-of-saving-my-soul school, my love-you-no-matter-what parents, and my great kick-ass sisters...all of my sisters... that's what it was like for me "Growing Up Hollywood."

If you feel like it, you can come along with me and find out what it was like to "Live and Work and Love Hollywood Style." Unless you're worn out and need to take a rest for awhile. I'll still be here waiting for you when you come back.

FIVE

Livin' Large in Hollywood

Let the Good Times Roll!

"Lisa, Lisa! You have to come right away! It's an emergency!" One of my tenants, Charlie Marion, was alternately ringing the bell and beating on my door in the middle of the night.

"Okay, okay. What's the big emergency?" I staggered half asleep to the door.

"You have to come up to my apartment right now. This is terrible!"

"Charlie, just tell me what your problem is." Charlie was standing there in his robe, he wasn't bleeding, and there were no cop cars driving up, so how bad could it be?

He insisted that I follow him to his apartment. When we got there, Charlie ran into the kitchen and threw open the refrigerator door.

"The light is out in my refrigerator, and I can't find anything," he wailed.

Oh, take me to your bosom, sweet Jesus! I got Charlie a flashlight and told him I'd fix the refrigerator light in the morning.

Charlie Marion had been a comedy writer for Abbott and Costello and was writing for a few TV shows (including *The Addams Family*) while he lived at the Beresford Apartments. It was unfortunate that he had already gotten divorced from Elena Verdugo, who starred in many B western and horror films, and who eventually played Robert Young's assistant in *Marcus Welby, M.D.* If Elena had been there, she probably could have found the flashlight for Charlie and he would have left me alone!

Charlie was a little "needy" in home repairs, but he was actually a very sweet guy who would take us girls to dinner periodically—always timed by when his residual checks came in. At the least, he was actually quite sane, which was a nice change from the tenant I had in there right before him: Ray Anthony, the band leader. Anthony was loony and only stayed in what became Charlie's apartment for two months. Maybe Anthony walked around the pool all day talking to himself because he'd just been divorced by Mamie Van Doren—a super-hot sex symbol. It's amazing how, as sex decreases, craziness increases in some guys.

I was in charge of burned-out refrigerator light bulbs because it was the early '60s and I was managing the Beresford Apartments at La Brea and Franklin in Los Angeles for my father. He had bought the building and asked Mike Mancuso and me to manage it for him. Mike wasn't too keen on the idea, but I was definitely on board with it. Our marriage was within a few feet of heading over the divorce cliff, and I could just feel that the Beresford would be the right spot for me to land.

Mike and I moved in and about two months later, Mike moved out. My dad was really worried about the split, but more because of the apartments than because of me. He knew I could take care of myself, but he was struggling with, "Now I have to find someone to manage the Beresford! Great!"

"No, you don't. I can handle it," I assured him.

"Loretta, you're a smart girl, but you're a girl. How can you keep the apartments rented, collect the rents, and keep up with the maintenance?"

"Just give me a chance at it, Dad. I won't let you down," I assured him. He did, and I did not—let him down.

I had been preparing to manage the Beresford alone since the minute we moved in anyway. Mike and I were so short-lived. He was a nice enough guy (most of the time), but I had really only married him to move out of my parents' house and declare my independence. Part of the problem with our marriage was that our whole relationship started with a misunderstanding and never got any better.

I had just had my nose fixed when I met Mike…I mean **just** had it fixed. I had bandages across my nose and two black eyes. I told him that my father beat me, but that if he ever met him, he shouldn't say anything or it might happen again. (How bad was I—talking that way about my wonderful father?) The misunderstanding was that Mike didn't know I was kidding. (I probably should have mentioned that at some point.)

We got married, and I continued my modeling and acting careers and became a showgirl, and Mike did…whatever kind of job my father helped him get. They were good jobs, and he brought home decent money, but Mike and I were really different people. While I was pursuing my lifelong interest, reading history books, Mike was reading comic books. While I was game to try whatever adventure lurked around the bend, he just wanted to sit at home…with his comic books. This was not going to work.

One of the more interesting parts of our marriage was our divorce. This was before the no-fault divorce law in California, so somebody had to be blamed for a breakup and somebody else had to swear to it. The headline on top of the second page of the *Herald Express* read "Flying Eggs Are No Yolk." (It must have been a slow news day.) The article explained (truthfully) that Mike had gotten mad about the way I was making his eggs, so he took a spatula and broke them. When I threw the eggs down the sink, Mike threw the pan across the room, grabbed me by the hair, sat on my chest, and beat on me. Gerri Nelson testified that she witnessed it all. (No, she wasn't there, but that's what friends do, isn't it? One tells the story and the other swears to it.) My divorce was granted and Mike was ordered to pay $50 a month alimony for 6 months and $1 a year after that. (I never got my money. Surprise.) The article was accompanied by a great photo of both Gerri and me. We both got calls for modeling from it. There's always a silver lining.

So there I was at the Beresford, sans Mike, and I had sworn to my father that I could do the job—even though I was a girl. The first order of business was to get all the units rented. I showed Dad that keeping the Beresford full wasn't too hard to do. Hell, there were only 18 units—I always knew 18 people who needed a great place to live!

I didn't just rent out the apartments, though; I "cast" the building. The first thing I did was to make it appealing to the kind of people I wanted to live and party with. I painted all the doors purple. I arranged to have four of our phones brought out to the pool, so none of my aspiring actors would miss an agent's call.

The Beresford cast included my friend Gerri naturally, along with an assortment of the soon-to-be famous, the wanna-be famous, and a few already famous. I also had the "extras" in our cast—a few gay guys, some transvestites and transsexuals, and some well-paid, high-class hookers. (Well, you can't have all A stars—you need a few extras sprinkled around for color.)

Those cross-dressers were really convenient to have around. If you needed some really glitzed-out accessories for a night on the town, you had more than just the girls' closets to check out. And it was always fun helping them put themselves together for their "biggest night of the year": Halloween— the holiday-of-choice for gays everywhere. I remember one Halloween when three of the gays downstairs needed to borrow clothes that would fit their friend, who just happened to be a huge Mexican. That guy must have been 6'4" and 260 pounds! We all almost busted a gut trying to get him into one of my Merry Widows! He looked like a sausage—skin was hanging out all over the place. But the guys were thrilled, and out to do the town they went. (I decided to let him keep that Merry Widow—I wasn't so keen on it after I saw what we'd shoved in there.)

Nope, no problems keeping the Beresford full. Almost overnight, it had become **the** place to live, especially because it was filled with really cute girls. My tenants came from everywhere: friends, family, casting calls, and referrals from my already-tenants. Most of my renters were already Hollywood girls, but there were a few California newcomers.

Answering a knock on my door one day, I found Susan Mintz and Sheila Kaplan and lots of suitcases. They said they were hoping that I had an apartment open because they had just arrived from Cleveland and were planning to be Hollywood stars. Susan said, "If we had stayed in Cleveland one more week, we would have committed suicide."

I suggested that since committing suicide in Cleveland was a little redundant it was a good thing they'd found their way to the Beresford.

Besides being gorgeous, Susan and Sheila could have been the poster girls for Jewish American Princesses, and they fit in immediately with the rest of our "cast of lovelies." Neither of the girls made it as stars, but while they were trying, we all had a ball together. And they eventually didn't do too badly in the marrying department. Susan Mintz married Bobby Banas, an incredible choreographer, dancer, and dance instructor. Anybody who was anybody took Banas' dancing classes. Sheila married Ken Scott (*Stopover Tokyo*) who was in serious demand for TV shows. I'm glad they didn't get married right away though—we would have missed too many fun times!

Then there was Deirdre Flynn—the youngest tenant I ever had and the one who has been around the most and the longest in my life. Deirdre was the daughter of Errol Flynn and his second wife, Nora Eddington, and she was 17 years old when she was dropped off at the Beresford. I mean literally "dropped off." After she and her mother got into a huge fight, Deirdre ran away and was hitchhiking down Laurel Canyon. Instead of some pervert picking her up (which could have easily happened), luck intervened and Fred "The Plumber," a well-known Hollywood detective, recognized her and got her off the street. Fred knew me (hell, everybody knew me!), so after listening to Deirdre's story, he brought her to the Beresford. Like I had turned into a damn rescue shelter? Fine...I put her on my couch (which was in between drop-ins right then) and eventually, I got her set up in her own place.

I couldn't turn Deirdre away—everybody knew what a rough deal she'd had being Errol Flynn's daughter. She was just a sweet girl who needed a better break than she'd gotten out of life so far. I mean—how would you have felt being a young teenager when your hotshot, swashbuckling, movie-star dad was publically fucking...a young teenager? And I thought my Immaculate Heart classmates were cruel to make fun of my nose? I didn't want to think about what Deirdre's "friends" did to her!

This reminds me...I need to tell you something. If you are a celebrity of any kind—Hollywood, politician, or even a big fish in your little pond—you shouldn't go around fucking people whose names are not listed on your Marriage Certificate! Besides not being the right thing to do, you are going to get caught. You think you won't? Read the paper! I repeat—you are going to get caught, and then your kids' friends are going to make fun of them. You do not want that. You do not want your 17 year old sleeping on some stranger's couch because of your headlines, do you? Okay, I'm sure you've got that. But to make sure, if you are already misbehaving, just go and send an email to your "misbehavee" right now and say,

"It's over. I do not want people to make fun of my kids." I'll still be here when you come back.

Of course, Errol was doing everybody right up to his death when Deirdre was 14. Many years after I met her, I asked her how she felt about her dad having so many affairs. Deirdre said, "My dad never had affairs. He didn't have anything romantic going on. That was not love with him. He just fucked people. But at least he didn't discriminate against anyone. Color or race, women or men—he'd fuck them all."

Everyone in Hollywood (actually, the rest of the world too) knew about Errol Flynn's reputation as a "seducer of all things moving." The expression "in like Flynn" was already being used by everybody when I met Deirdre. *Did you know that phrase came from Errol Flynn? He had an all-female jury for his trial for statutory rape of two under-age girls in the early '40s. I don't how it happened, but people who were there said he flirted with the jury so well (in the courtroom!) that they let him off. Maybe like O.J. Simpson when he was flipping his tie and acting all cutesy at his trial. Remember that? Anyway..."in like Flynn" means that you are untouchable—you've got things so locked up that, no matter what happens, you'll come out on top. Isn't that cool? You just got a little "gift with purchase"—a vocabulary lesson. Stay tuned. I think there's a history lesson coming up too.*

One thing that Hollywood didn't know was that Errol was crazy about his kids. I drove Deirdre up to Laurel Canyon to get her things when it was obvious that she wasn't going back home. What she was most concerned about was a large box of letters from her father. He had written her almost every day whenever he was on location. They were all two- or three-page, handwritten letters that Deirdre would re-read many times a week. She often mentioned how her father would call her from all over the country just to say goodnight to her. Deirdre had no illusions about her father's outrageous behavior, but she held on to what a daughter really needs and values. She knew that, in spite of everything else, her father loved her.

Not too long after Deirdre showed up and before I got her into her place (vacancies didn't come around fast in my Beresford), who shows up? Beverly Aadland! Dear God, what have I done to piss you off again, that you should dump two of them on me at the same time? Deirdre was a little screwed up at the time, but Beverly? She was in a world of hurt!

To catch you up, here's a short, Hollywood trashy history lesson. Beverly met Errol Flynn when he sought her out on a Warner Brothers lot when she was 15. He seduced her and continued their relationship until he had a fatal heart attack in Vancouver when he was 50. She was 17 at that time—but a very old 17, having been Errol's lover and companion for two years. Beverly went home to her mother's immediately after Errol died, where her nightmare continued. She was raped by one of her mother's friends during an out-of-control party. Her rapist accidentally shot himself with his own gun afterwards and died from his wound. (That asshole had nothing going for him: evil, stupid, and a bad shot.) Beverly was taken away from her mother and put into foster care until she was 18. How terrible was that? Going from traveling all over the world with Flynn—champagne, caviar, and expensive jewelry—to a rape victim in a foster home in one year?

In 1961, Beverly's piece-of-trash mother wrote a book (*The Big Love*) without Beverly's permission, which was the story of her daughter and Errol Flynn. Now, why would a mother do something like that? Anyway, Beverly was super pissed, took off, and went in search of Deirdre, which is why she showed up on my doorstep. When she stepped inside my apartment, Beverly had the clothes on her back and $18 in her pocket. Great. What was I supposed to do? I sure couldn't turn her away.

I gave Beverly some fresh clothes and dragged some big pillows and blankets into the living room, and she immediately curled up and slept for 14 hours straight. As soon as she woke up, I told her that I couldn't keep her around forever and that she was going to have to figure something out. She hung around, just being quiet and staying to herself for a few weeks, and then handed me a piece of paper with the name of a minister at a mission in San Fernando Valley. She started crying and asked if I could take her there.

After I called and verified that the guy was really a minister and that the place was really a mission, I drove her up there with Deirdre hugging her in the back seat and Beverly crying the whole way. I handed her over to the minister who was very quiet and had kind, I'll-look-after-her eyes, and Deirdre and I drove away. Beverly had on the same clothes she'd worn to my house and $50 (of my money) in her pocket.

And with that, it was back to the Beresford to take care of my other tenants who, thankfully, were not nearly as fucked up!

With Deirdre in place at the Beresford, there was one more central player in our cast. She may have been 17 when she arrived, but she was a lot older than most of us in life experience. She fit right in. And more fun people kept coming to the Beresford.

I'm not sure how or even when Cher arrived, but at some point, there she was. You'd think that Cher arriving to live and party with all of us would have been a big deal, right? But it wasn't—because she wasn't THE Cher then; she was just a great-looking sessions singer who was doing what so many others were at the time—looking for her big break.

She may have been "only" Cher—"that girl who sings all the time"—but she was more than welcome at the Beresford. She was the same girl then that she is now: generous, fun, and a really kind person—besides being a real knock-out girl who loved to party. She was great to have around, except for all that singing! That's all she did—in her apartment, sitting around the pool, dumping her trash—she was always singing. Usually it would just be some small part of a song over and over and over again. When I'd heard the same thing like 100 times, I'd holler, "Hey, Cher! Will you just shut the fuck up?" She'd just laugh and keep singing. Yes, I really did tell Cher to stop singing. Who knew? (A year or so later, after she'd become THE Cher, she met my sister Joey, and they've remained good friends for 40 years. Joey called me up the night after they met and asked me if I really used to tell Cher to, "Shut the fuck up," because she was singing too much. I tried to lie my way out of it, but Joey knew better, and she just started laughing. She said Cher brought it up as soon as she heard "Malouf" and was (thankfully!) laughing about it too.)

During the Beresford days, wherever Cher was—there was Sonny. Sonny lived next door to us and would bring big pots of his homemade spaghetti when he'd come over to hang out around the pool. That guy could do more than just sing. He could also really cook!

Cher was more often at Sonny's than she was in her own apartment though, unless her mother was coming to visit. Then we'd run over to Sonny's, throw her clothes out the window to each other, run back to her place, and fill the closet. When her mother left, we'd bring the clothes back to Sonny's. Back and forth, back and forth—Cher's mother came to visit too many times! (Sure helps keep your figures in great shape, though, when you're a "clothes runner.")

I stayed in touch with Cher off and on over the years after we all left the Beresford and gave her a baby shower for Chastity at the Beverly Hills Hotel in 1969. It was a huge party, but a lot of it is a blur today. I was the hostess; I had stuff to do that day. There were almost 200 people at the party, but the gift (and guest) I remember the best was an antique wooden snow sleigh that Mama Cass had filled with presents. It was wonderful...I really wanted to take that one home with me! I don't remember what I gave Cher for her shower gift—maybe a party for 200 people.

Our friendship continued through the '70s when I'd go to her skating parties in San Fernando Valley. By that time, Cher and many of her other friends had too much "celebrity" to be able to go out with "regular" people and really enjoy themselves. So she'd rent a roller rink one night a week for disco roller-skating parties. They were invitation-only, which meant that I'd get calls from people like Joanna Cassidy and Jane Seymour who knew I was going and wanted me to get them in. Sometimes yes, and sometimes...no. (They had to catch me on a "generous" day.)

I recently saw Cher after one of her shows at Caesars in Vegas. She's still Cher: kind, generous, and gorgeous. She has a few more years on her, like the rest of us. But on her—who can tell and who even cares? She's an icon...and still a friend.

Cher, Susan, Sheila, Gerri, Deirdre, and me—we were the core of the Beresford girls, but our cast was filled in by other great "players" that would move and a few drop-ins. Sometimes the drop-ins would drop right onto my couch until they could either get their own apartments or move on to somewhere else. One of those was a beautiful model named Sue Barton.

Sue was Jeff Chandler's mistress when he died from a botched surgery for a herniated disc in 1961. The doctors nicked an artery, and Jeff needed emergency surgery. He got 55 pints of blood during that second surgery, along with another 20 pints after that. You can guess at the size of that malpractice suit! Anyway, Sue was wrecked about Jeff's death and came to stay on my couch for awhile. She did seem to recover from her trauma pretty fast. One night, I was more than a little irritated when I got home and saw that my full length Black Diamond mink coat was not in the closet. Hours later, Sue came sashaying home in my mink! I would have let her wear it if she would have asked, but you just don't grab a girl's mink without asking! (Oh well, it was stolen years later in a robbery of my El Centro apartment anyway. Easy come, easy...not.)

Another really popular drop-in was Nicky Blair. Although he was in like 100 TV shows and almost that many movies, he became really famous for his Hollywood restaurants, which were the hot spots for every celebrity for years. It was great timing for us that Nicky was still preparing to get into the food business and needed some "food critics" to try out his recipes. He'd show up with big platters of chicken piccata and osso bucco. The crowd around the pool would swell considerably when the word went around that Nicky was going to feed us. Those would be the nights when we'd pull out the super-clean trash can I had marked just for these occasions and drag it to the pool. We'd fill it with ice, champagne, and spiced peaches and ladle it out into our crystal champagne flutes. (Hello, Betty Wittkins!) So what if we had glass at the pool? I was the manager…we could do anything that I wanted to!

It is a damn good thing that Nicky (and sometimes Sonny Bono) were doing the cooking. When someone would ask any of us girls what we were making for dinner, the answer usually was "reservations."

Nope—keeping my Beresford full was not a big problem. During one period when there was a writer's strike in Hollywood, some of my aspiring actors were having problems getting parts, so they moved on and it looked like I could have some vacancies. Oh no—I can't! I'd told my dad that I could keep the building filled, and I was damn well going to do that!

That's when I let a few well-paid hookers into the Beresford. They just needed a "day place" to crash. They skulked around during the day, and paid their rent on time…except for one of them. I got tired real fast of chasing her for her check. Okay, I knew how to get my money. (My dad's money, actually.)

All hookers kept a "Date Book" with all the vital information about their customers—like price, specific requests, and names. Everything was clearly laid out, but the names were coded—I think you needed the Hooker's Guide to Johns or a Captain Midnight Magic Decoder Ring to figure them out. The preferred storage place for the Date Book was in the freezer wrapped in waxed paper. I knew where my delinquent tenant's book was, and I had a buyer for that book—who obviously had the Magic Decoder Ring to match the code to the name to the price to the kinky stuff. And, I knew where to find a little black book to match my hooker tenant's: Schwab's in Hollywood for $1.19.

I went to my overdue hooker's apartment, helped myself to her Date Book, and ran downstairs to my apartment to copy everything into my new black book as fast as I could. No copiers—this was by hand—and she had a really good-sized clientele! I had to hurry because my buyer was waiting in the parking garage, and I needed to get the original back into the freezer. The last notation in the book read: "OB33, $200, dress like schoolgirl and knock on door. Don't go in. No fucking. Just stand there—will jack off."

Okay, even though I was rushing, I had to stop and think about that one for a minute. I still had my Immaculate Heart High School uniform. I was wishing that I knew who OB33 was. I'd stand at anybody's door and have him do...whatever...to himself for $200. Another lost opportunity for "personal enrichment."

I handed over the copy of the Date Book, got $3,000, and ran back up to deposit the original in the hooker's freezer. The next day, I gave my dad $125 for her month's rent and told my grateful tenant that I was going to let her stay for one more month until she got back on her feet—or back on her back, whatever it took for her to get the next rent check. I only had $1.19 invested in this venture, so I had lots left over. I pondered about what to do with it. I didn't ponder too long though. A great night on the town for all my friends, a new fox jacket, and a pair of Courreges go-go boots took care of my extraordinary profit.

After I got married (again) and moved out of the Beresford, David Marks (of the Beach Boys) bought the Beresford and had his parents manage it for him. But they couldn't keep it rented and moved on. Sorry for them, but it wasn't that hard …you just had to be a little creative and put together the right "cast."

The renting and the collecting at the Beresford didn't cause me problems, but I wasn't too keen on some of the maintenance issues. Although I could handle most of them myself, I had better things to do with my time than change burned out refrigerator lights, have locks re-keyed, and put on new cabinet handles. I remember getting calls from several tenants one morning at some ungodly hour (like 10:00 a.m.) that there was no hot water. I staggered down to the basement and lit a cigarette while I was looking at the water heater. That was not a great move. A blue flame shot out and threw me off my feet into a rolled up carpet that was down there. Damn! Maybe this wasn't a girl's job.

During the Beresford years, we didn't do drugs and we didn't even drink a lot. (Well, except for the champagne-filled trash can nights.) We were fueled by other highs—sex (lots of that) and the applause that most of us heard in our day gigs, acting and modeling.

Speaking of lots of sex…that not only went on pretty well non-stop at the Beresford, but we extended our sexual range to the neighborhood as well. Ricky Nelson lived just four blocks from us. Everybody (yes, me too) at the Beresford drove (or sometimes even walked) the four blocks to Ricky's house to get laid. He was a doll who looked like a 16 year old even though he wasn't. We all felt real "naughty" (because he looked like such a kid), and Ricky was wonderfully accommodating with (thankfully) a quick recovery time.

I remember one day when one of the girls said she was going to "get a Ricky," and Gerri said, "You probably should wait awhile. I just got back from there, and I don't think he has anything left right now."

"Damn, Gerri!" said the girl. "Didn't your mother teach you to share?"

Gerri replied with, "Sure she did, but not Ricky Nelson's dick!"

Sometimes my maintenance tasks extended to repairs on my tenants too. Once at 2:30 in the morning, there was a knock on my door—again! It was Nate, one of my quiet, 50-ish tenants, who rarely said much more than hello every night on his way out to the local bars he liked to frequent. Now, there he was, with only a towel wrapped around his waist. No shirt, no shoes...just the towel, and it was a cheap, small one, too.

"I need money. I need to pay the cab," he was hollering frantically.

"What happened to you?" I asked.

Nate shouted, "It's a long story...I need to pay the cab!"

"Nate, are you okay?" I replied. "Where are your clothes—and your money?"

Now he was getting louder, "It's just a long story. Give me money for the cab!"

I went down and paid the cab myself. I didn't need almost-naked Nate going down to the street again. When I returned, he was sitting on my couch, looking wrecked.

"Okay, straighten out that damn towel and tell me what happened," I told him.

Well, quiet and not-too-smart Nate had met a girl that he thought was "nice," and she'd taken him to a hotel room. When he came out of the bathroom, she was gone and so was everything else—his clothes, his shoes, his watch, and his wallet. I didn't have to lecture Nate about the business model of low-priced hookers. I think he had figured it out.

The Beresford Apartments became my "gold standard" for where and how I wanted to live, but they were a little exhausting. Remember—I was going back and forth to perform in Vegas, working in lots of TV shows, and modeling all over L.A.—all at the same time!

Speaking of working in Hollywood...

Working 24/7: Hollywood Style

"You're sure I'm going to play the girl next door? Come on...I don't have to be some Greek or Mexican or Middle Eastern chick? Just who finally believes that I look like a regular white girl? Remember me? I'm the one you hired out to the real estate company to be their black contestant in the Miss Black L.A. pageant. Which I did not win, by the way—big surprise. So now I'm a white girl?"

I was questioning my agent because I had never played the girl next door before, but he was now telling me that I was going to be Burl Ives' daughter on Burl's TV special. I knew I looked a little exotic for Midwest America, but I think part of the "non-lily-white parts" issue was my agent, Fred Ishimoto. I should have known better than to sign up with a guy whose client list was made up entirely of Asians... and me.

Throughout my acting career, I must have appeared in 50 TV shows and movies. But you wouldn't know that today. If you google Lisa Medford or Lisa Britton or Loretta Malouf, you'll find out that I was Lily Belle in *American Hot Wax*. I'm also listed as the assistant accountant for the *Monsters* TV series and production auditor for *My Mom's a Werewolf*. (Those last two jobs were 20 years later, however, when I had stepped behind the camera.) But all my other acting gigs? They just don't show up.

Actually, that pisses me off. So much for imdb.com (Internet Movie Database) being the "single source of truth" about who was in which movie and TV show and when. It's not that my parts were so small...well, yes, maybe it's partly because my parts were pretty small. But I wasn't even an extra—I had real parts! I belonged to SAG, AFTRA, AGVA, and the Director's Guild of America! You know how much that is in dues? Too damn much! I didn't even belong to the fucking SEG (the extra's union.) So, where are my credits? Oh well, I don't care that much anymore, I guess. I still get residual checks from *Nevada Smith* and *The Beverly Hillbillies* and *American Hot Wax*, and I have my pictures with the stars I've acted with. Actually, I guess I didn't care that much back then either. I had no visions of stardom. My objectives were to work and be with my friends and buy great clothes. And I just wanted to have fun. (I figure Cindy Lauper must have written that song for me.)

A short list of the TV shows I was actually in includes (one to several episodes each) *77 Sunset Strip, Maverick, Roaring 20's, Klondike,* and *Sugarfoot.* I was in high demand for celebrity shows like the *George Gobel Show, The Beverly Hillbillies, The Jonathan Winters Show,* and *You Bet Your Life,* with Groucho Marx. Sometimes I just did the shows once, but for others, I was in several episodes.

I appeared in lots of stars' specials too: Dean Martin's, Frank Sinatra's, Bob Hope's. So there, IMDb! Get your facts straight!

Some of the shows are great memories. One time, the writers for *You Bet Your Life* thought I looked like Groucho's ex-wife, Barbara, and thought it would be funny to spoof Groucho by having me be the stuffed duck. (Short TV history lesson here—whenever a contestant said the Secret Word, a duck would come out of the ceiling and hand over $100.)

I had to get to the studio early so they could do my makeup and stuff me into my cage and raise me up to the ceiling before the live audience showed up. Great...once again, up in the air, and I'm afraid of heights! I thought a few Life Savers would comfort me...maybe save my life... so I popped a few in my mouth before I got in the cage. It didn't occur to me that I might get caught sucking on candy. I figured, it was probably going to be awhile before I heard the Secret Word. But no, right away, some damn fool said the Word, the bell rang, and down I went. Okay...I can do this. I can't just swallow the Life Savers or I'll choke to death right on the show, and I can't get caught chewing on them. It's okay—I can just walk over, hand the money to Groucho, smile nice, and get back in the cage. That's all I'm supposed to do.

Groucho was cracking up because I was definitely not his usual duck. After handing over the money, I got back in the cage and headed back up to the ceiling, but before I got far, Groucho said, "Bring her back down." So, down I went again, desperately trying to suck the life out of the Life Savers. Groucho wanted to visit with me on air, which was not in the script! No, no talking, please!

"So, what's your name? Where do you come from? Did you always want to be a duck?"

Groucho asked me stupid stuff like that. I don't remember exactly how that conversation went because I was trying to smile, answer, and swallow Life Savers before I opened my mouth and spewed them all over him. *Do you remember seeing that show with Groucho Marks talking to his live duck? If you do, that was me, and now you know why I had puffy cheeks.*

Groucho and his duck, Lisa

The Beverly Hillbillies was another hoot to work on, but getting the part in the show is the event I remember the most.

One day I was shopping in Hollywood and wearing my "wealthy Hollywood wife" outfit: a camel's hair suit with a leopard skin collar and a matching leopard hat that covered all my hair. I stopped shopping just long enough to call my agent and he was frantic. "I've been looking for you. Get over to *The Beverly Hillbillies* producer's offices at General Services Studios right away. They're looking for belly dancers, and I told them you were coming!" Belly dancers? Okay, maybe I wasn't dressed for a belly-dancing audition, and I'd never even tried belly dancing, but those details didn't hold me back.

When I showed up, the *Hillbillies* people said right away that I didn't look like a belly dancer. They were just going to turn their backs and ignore me. I don't think so! So, I took off my hat, and my long hair came tumbling down. Then I pulled up my silk blouse, pulled down the waistband of my skirt, and pointed to my belly button.

"Do you see that? My dancing name is Zenobia, and that's the most famous navel in the world."

Are you wondering how I came up with that? Zenobia was (is) a gourmet nut company, and I had just bought two bags of pistachios before I got to the audition. It was good for me that the Hillbillies *people were not nut lovers.*

They looked at "the most famous navel in the world," and not only did I get the part, but they asked me to choreograph the dance, since I was the famous Zenobia. Not a problem. I called on one of my dancer friends, and she taught me four basic moves. (Damn, that belly dancing is hard work—I think I lost an inch around my waist just rehearsing!) I taught the other dancers, and we were the Sheik's Girls. Another kick... and more applause for Lisa Zenobia.

For one of my appearances on *The Jonathan Winters Show*, I was supposed to model Rudy Gernreich's monokini—the first topless swimsuit, which came out in 1964. What a topic for chatter that was—even though they were butt-ugly and not many people were wearing them. Monokinis were immediately banned all over the U.S. and even in St. Tropez! (I don't think the French banned them because they were topless. They were probably just too ugly for French fashion standards.)

Being banned didn't stop the Condor Club in North San Francisco from deciding to be the first topless bar and putting its dancers in monokinis, though. *Surely you remember Carol Doda, don't you? She was the first topless dancer (in a bar) to wear a monokini. Almost a year later, she was arrested for indecency. A year later! Guess the cops in San Francisco had poor eyesight. It took them a year of staring at her to decide if it was really indecent?*

The Jonathan Winters Show writers prepared a hilarious skit with Jonathan as Maudie Frickert (his old lady character) and me in a "modified" monokini. The swimsuit had been cleaned up for TV by Don Feld, the famous costume designer who also did the costumes for *Viva Las Vegas* and *Diamonds are Forever.* Revising the monokini was not his best work, however. Don "designed" a band of black fabric that stretched across my chest. The audience members were supposed to use their imaginations. It must have worked for them though because the catcalls and applause were over the top! (I could hardly wait to get that damn thing off. It was smashing my boobs so hard, I was afraid they'd never bounce back. They did.)

The revamped monokini and Maudie Frickert

Another Vegas/Hollywood crossover happened when I worked on *The Frank Sinatra Show* in Hollywood. Even though I had no respect for him, Frank's money spent the same as everybody else's so... Working that show, I found out right away that Mr. Arrogant-Everybody-Do-My-Biding Sinatra wasn't any nicer in Hollywood than he was in Vegas. I was dancing in his show and sat around in full makeup and costumes (with all the rest of the cast) for six hours waiting for Mr. Wonderful to appear. Asshole.

Along with my TV appearances, I was getting calls like crazy for ads and photo shoots for magazines, calendars...it seemed like I was everywhere!

I got a call to do a Schlitz beer shoot for a billboard. "That's cool," I thought—I'll be up in the air without being afraid! There was one problem when I showed up, though. I had recently bleached my hair blond for some other job and the

Schlitz people were expecting a black-haired, Spanish-looking girl. Okay, not a problem. I didn't have a wig with me, but I knew that two blocks down there was a pharmacy that sold spray hair dye. I ran down there, sprayed like crazy, and came back—black-headed. (It took awhile to wash that shit out!) They dressed me in a ruffly, red dancer's outfit and handed me castanets. It took longer to spray my hair than it did to get the shots, so I was out of there quickly, but I was really excited to see the finished billboard.

When they told me it was up in some crappy Mexican neighborhood, I wondered what the deal was. When I saw the billboard, though, I knew. The damn thing was all in Spanish! It said something like, "Famous Mexican dancer, Carmelita Lopez, loves Schlitz beer!" Actually, I thought it was pretty funny. Zenobia, Carmelita, Loretta, Lisa…call me whatever you want. Just call.

I was in so many magazines that I've lost count. I've already mentioned that I was a "staple" for *Man's Magazine*, but I don't think I included *Playboy* (multiple times…not a Playmate though), and magazines that you may not have heard of.

I recently saw a piece I'd torn out of some forgettable magazine. The scrap of the magazine that I have just has a very provocative picture of me, lying topless on what looks like a kitchen counter with a fur wrapped around me—but not hiding the good parts. Right below the picture it reads, "Miss Mancuso's curves are Egyptian in origin—but won't remind you of plane geometry." Egyptian? There are just a few words from the accompanying article right above the picture that I can make out: *mathematics, equation,* and *triangle.* Now, just how much weed was that art director smoking when he thought, "I know! We should put a topless model into that article about geometry! That will really spice it up!" Okay, worked for me. I'm sure I got paid.

"Were you ever diagnosed with ADD when you were a kid?" A friend asked me that a few years ago.

"What? No! Hey girl, think this out. We didn't know what hell ADD was when I was growing up. I didn't have a deficiency in my attention—I just redefined multitasking. I didn't do a lot of little things at the same time. I did a lot of big things at the same time!"

What was she thinking? ADD? I had to pay really good attention to keep track of everything I was doing at the same time. That's why I had big-ass calendar books for every year. (Good thing I held on to most of those books all these years. Who could remember all that today? Not even me...and I was the one doing it!)

What I was doing was managing the Beresford, working as a showgirl, acting and modeling, and starting my wig company and my antique store (and probably some other shit that I've forgotten), and I was also getting divorced and married again and being romanced by some fabulous guys (and a few flat tires).

You might remember some of the men that I shared my life and my bed with: the movie star Cary Grant, the director Don Medford, and the composer, Ladi Staidl.

Six

"Just" Cary Grant

"Sweet Lisa, I have a proposition for you. If you can bring me proof that you're three months pregnant, I'll marry you and you'll be set for life."

For one of the few times in my life, no words could come out of my mouth. Cary Grant and I were in a seriously fancy restaurant having a great, quiet dinner together until he laid that one on me. A baby…he wants a baby? "Set for life"… well, those words didn't sound bad. But…a baby? I don't think so. Not Lisa who never left home without her birth control pills. I was overwhelmed and embarrassed, and my mind quickly went to, "What would I tell my parents?" They'd disown me if I got pregnant when I wasn't married, and my family was more important to me than Cary Grant.

I couldn't even come up with an answer, so I just smiled a little Audrey Hepburn smile and looked down. "That's okay, Lisa. I'm sure you'll need time to think about this. I certainly want you to want to have my baby." Oh, dear. I didn't need time to think about that. That just wasn't going to happen.

I don't know because I wasn't there, but I have to believe that Cary made Dyan Cannon the same offer. "Have my baby and I'll marry you, and you'll be set for life." Dyan must have taken that deal. Their daughter, Jennifer Grant, was born "prematurely." Sure she was. I'll lay large money that they eloped as soon as Dyan showed Cary the proof he needed.

When Cannon left Cary 10 months after Jennifer was born, one of her complaints was that he spanked her when she disobeyed. I don't know about that. I wasn't there to see that either, but he certainly never came close to spanking me. Maybe I didn't get spanked because it never occurred to me to "disobey" him. Cary was classy and sophisticated and gentlemanly. He made you want to be the way he was, and how he expected you to be. He liked quiet nights together, curled up in bed and watching TV or just reading together. He liked "calm and quiet," and I liked him, so I was calm and quiet. (Damn near killed me sometimes, though.)

Parts of my vocabulary just seemed to alter themselves when I was around Cary. The "F" word, or any other bad word, did not come out of my mouth when I was with him. He had the old-world, "act like a gentleman around a lady" manners. Dropping an "F" bomb around Cary Grant? I don't think so! He was so "Cary Grant" all the time.

Soon after we started dating, we were reading an article that was proclaiming his great acting skills. I asked, "Cary, how do you do that? How do you act?"

"Dear Lisa, I don't act. I'm just Cary Grant. They give me a different name, but I'm still just Cary Grant." **Just** Cary Grant? That was good enough, obviously! *North by Northwest* had come out just before I met him in 1960, and Cary was one of the, if not **the**, biggest movie star in Hollywood. **Just** Cary Grant?

Cary also shared this insight (and opinion of himself) with me: "You have to be either a bigger-than-life personality, or a bigger-than-life talent. I have the personality, but that doesn't mean I have the talent."

While the rest of the world was calling him one of the greatest talents anyone had ever seen, I think that he didn't really believe that he was an actor, that he didn't value his movies as his legacy. Cary was on a quest for the kind of immortality that comes from giving your name and genes to children. It took me many years to look at all the pieces of our relationship and realize that everything about our time together was about baby making.

"Cary Grant and Lisa" started when my agent called me one afternoon, all excited. "Cary Grant wants to meet you. I was at the Studio showing your pictures around, and Cary wants you to go by his bungalow at Universal Studios."

"Do you think I can go next week?" I asked. "I'm pretty tied up right now."

"Are you crazy? It's Cary Grant! He thinks you look like Sophia Loren in that photo you had taken for your engagement to Mancuso. Get your butt over there!" My agent had a greater sense of urgency than I did, obviously. Sure, I knew Cary Grant was a major player, but I knew lots of big stars. Okay, fine. I'll get over there.

Everyone in Hollywood knew that Cary Grant was head over heels in love with Sophia Loren and had been for years. He'd fallen for her during their filming of *The Pride and the Passion.* They'd had a hot affair, but after the shooting was over, so was the affair. Unfortunately for Cary, Sophia had already found Carlo Ponti, who proved to be the love of her life. Because of Carlo, Sophia had wanted her romance with Cary to end, but that's not what he had in mind. A year later, she complained to Melville Shavelson, the director of *Houseboat*, that Cary wouldn't stop chasing her and wouldn't believe that she could be in love with Carlo Ponti. Shavelson had to tell Cary firmly to "knock it off and move on." For awhile, that whole deal was the talk of the town, but neither Cary's nor Sophia's reputation had suffered over the almost-a-scandal. They were Cary and Sophia, after all! They could pretty well do whatever they wanted. Hollywood had a short memory when it came to scandals anyway, especially when they were about people who made the studios so much money.

That Cary Grant thought I looked like his true love worked for me. I figured I'd probably get a good part out of him because of that. No movie part came out of our first meeting, but several years of being with Cary did. Actually, he never offered me a part in the picture he was working on, or in any of his other pictures. I never asked him because I cared about him. It was more important for me to be loved than to get another part. I never used our relationship to further my career. In fact, I would often not even give my name when we'd go out to parties together. I didn't need his spotlight—I was happy to be with him while he was in it.

Yes, there was a pretty big age difference between us. I was 23 and he was 57. One of my sisters asked, "What are you trying to do—marry our father?"

I didn't think so, but what would have been wrong with that, anyway? Our father and Cary Grant were a lot alike.

The picture that stole Cary Grant's heart

They both respected women and treated us really well. They were strong and kind and smart and rich. "I could do a lot worse than marrying our father," I replied. (And actually, I did do a lot worse. That's coming up too.)

I was still married to Mike Mancuso when I starting dating Cary, but Mike and I were at "roommate-only" status by then. It did kind of freak out Mike when Cary showed up at our apartment to pick me up. But what was he going to do—deck Cary Grant? I don't think so. Mike moved out soon after I started seeing Cary, although Cary's arrival had nothing to do with Mike's departure. By the time I starting dating Cary, Mike was "not relevant."

Our dates were…like Cary was. He wasn't into flashy or "Hollywood" in his dates, or in any part of his personal life. We did go to Hollywood parties and nice restaurants, like La Scala, occasionally, but it was really a hassle to go out. When we were in a public restaurant, we had to eat in a hidden corner in a dark place so that Cary could actually get through his meal. Too many times, he'd be lifting his fork but it wouldn't make it to his mouth because some star-struck fan would grab his arm to ask for an autograph. I don't know how he maintained his cool through those kinds of attacks, but he did every time. When the fan would finally leave our table, I'd be upset for him, but Cary would remind me, "They think that Cary Grant is special, and as long as they do…then Cary Grant always will be."

Dating Cary taught me an important lesson early in my budding career as an actress. Do not become a celebrity! It makes people do ugly things around you, and it controls your whole life.

That's when I vowed that I would never sacrifice my life for "celebrity." The only celebrity status I ever wanted was to walk into my bank and have them stand up and salute.

Cary was gorgeous and fun, and cheap, and a boring lover. But okay….that man was pure e-l-e-g-a-n-c-e, and that made me overlook his nickel-rubbing tendencies and his same, tired routine in bed. He never "courted me," and he wasn't particularly romantic. Today, I don't even remember kissing him. I'm sure we must have kissed, but it couldn't have been particularly earth moving. I don't recall any "sit on the couch, nibble on your lover's lips, and stare soulfully into her eyes" times. When Cary was ready for "love," it was "sex," and he got down to business. Our lovemaking was never spontaneous—there was no "pleasure fucking." He wanted me to be how he wanted me at parties, at restaurants, and in bed too. One night, I got a little friskier and started moving around while we were making love.

"Now, now, dear girl, you don't have to break the slats," he said. "Just lie there and think happy thoughts."

Hmmm...okay. I could do that. But I complained to my friend Gerri that Cary got into bed like he was "going to work." Now, I understand that he was. He was on a mission to build his legacy—that happy ending with a baby. I probably should have seen earlier how it all fit together, but I was busy living my life...and it was a good one!

In bed or out, Cary was all about baby making. He was asking me all the time about my periods. He'd get real amorous right in between them, and then he'd check again the next month. I never, ever told him about my always-close-to-me packet of birth control pills! I knew that would be the end of Cary and Lisa, and I wasn't willing to let it end—for awhile.

I understand there's a "tell-all" book that came out a few years ago that claims Cary Grant had a really small dick. I don't know who the author was sleeping with, or what kind of fucked-up ruler she used to measure, but believe me when I tell you….about eight inches **without** a hard-on is not small! I don't remember just how large that translated to when he was excited. As I mentioned, Cary got right to business, and I was busy "thinking happy thoughts." Maybe she got confused because his spike was good but his hammer was a little light. Cary just did not have an ass. It is harder to drive a railroad spike with a tack hammer, but still…Cary Grant had a little dick? Not. (*I'm not mentioning the book or the author because she pissed me off bad-mouthing Cary. If you figure out who she was anyway…please don't buy her book.*)

There were a few rumors floating around back then (and there still are) that Cary went both ways sexually. Because Cary and Randolph Scott lived together off and on, there was talk that they were a couple. But frankly, that kind of "crossing over" wasn't a huge deal in those days. A movie star's sexuality was just mildly interesting and something to put in the gossip columns when it was a slow news day. We just kind of figured back then that "Big Star = Big Appetite." The bigger the star—the more they got by with. (*Now, I'm not advocating that you should follow that model of "big appetite." Remember—we didn't have scary diseases back then. "Protected sex" meant that you locked the door so no one could walk in on you while you were doing it at a party. Today, you'd better wrap your whole body in industrial-strength Saran Wrap.*)

I sure didn't care if Cary was bisexual or not. When he was making love to me, I was the only other person there. That was good enough. Even though my "job" was to "think happy thoughts," his job was to give me those happy thoughts—and he did that well.

Cary's decision about whether or not I should be his breeder of choice extended to checking out my gene pool too. He was really interested in meeting my family and wanted to go with me to dinner at my parent's house the first year that we were together. When I called my mother to ask if I could bring him, even she was a little speechless. She'd lived around stars for years and years, but even with her, and the rest of my family...this was Cary Grant! He came to dinner, and I noticed that he was carefully checking out my parents, and my sisters. Of course, they were carefully checking him out too.

Cary had brought some wine to dinner and was opening a bottle when he cut himself on the corkscrew. My mother quickly handed him a linen napkin to stop the bleeding. We all cracked up when my sister Joey asked, "Can I have that when you're finished? I want real movie star blood."

Cary did have some issues that weren't really obvious on the surface. He really believed that he was "just" Cary Grant, that his image was all he had going for him. I certainly didn't spend my time dissecting the psychological profiles of my lovers, but it didn't take much dissection to know that Cary was more than a little insecure about his image. Part of that evidence was that he actively sought out ways to cope with his self-image concerns.

I met Cary as his marriage to Betsy Drake was winding down. Even though they had lived apart for some time when I started dating him, her influence in one area was still evident. While they were together, Betsy had introduced Cary to LSD, which was legal in the early '60s and was touted as a treatment for all kinds of psychological issues. While we were dating, Cary was still seeking ways to kill his demons.

One night, I was looking for something in the glove compartment of his Rolls Royce and found a small vial of liquid. When

I asked him what it was, Cary responded quickly. "Just put that away, dear girl. That's LSD. You don't need that. You're not messed up....you're just perfect the way you are. You don't have problems; I do. That's something that I need to have."

Cary may have been insecure about who Cary was, but whoever he thought Cary was, he was interested in guarding that identity.

While we were dating, Cary hired a new butler, a good-looking German guy named Ken. Ken really seemed to be doing a great job for Cary, preparing and laying out his clothes, making his personal appointments, keeping the wine cellar stocked, bringing him (and me) breakfast in bed. I commented on Ken's good work one day and said that I figured Cary would want to keep him around for a long time. (He had seemed to go through household help really fast.) Cary said, "No, he probably won't last. In about a year, he'll start thinking that he's Cary Grant, and then he'll have to leave."

Less than a year later, I was at Cary's and I noticed that Ken was gone, so I asked what happened. Cary told me, "I had to let him go. After he made my toast, he picked it up and ate it himself. He thought he was me."

I remember another evening when Cary's fear about identify theft popped right up—literally popped up. We were curled up in bed watching David Janssen play Richard Diamond. Sometime during the show, I remarked, "David Janssen sounded kind of like you when he said that!"

Cary was furious. He started doing a "Tom Cruise"— jumping up and down on the bed. "He is not Cary Grant! There's only one Cary Grant, and that's me! I'm sick of people trying to be Cary Grant!" He was so riled up and mad at me for bringing up the comparison, that he wouldn't talk to me for hours. I made a mental note not to say that anyone looked like or sounded like or thought they were Cary Grant!

I asked Cary once if he was guarding his stuff—like all his white boxer shorts and shirts and towels—by putting a CG monogram on everything. Was it to recover the stuff if it got stolen, or did he just need to remind himself that he was **the** "CG"? He wasn't amused.

Those kinds of events (Ken's leaving, being upset with David Janssen, taking LSD) gave me the clues that Cary needed the most stroking above his belt buckle. I sure don't want to make it sound as though he was some kind of emotional wreck, because he certainly was not. Cary was fun to be around, and that's why I kept seeing him (although I also kept taking those birth control pills).

Hanging out at Cary's house was really a delight. Although I was there a lot, I never moved in. Cary Grant or not, we didn't go on a date one day and move in the next in those days. (Today, people want to bring a U-Haul with their crap in it to the second date.) Cary had a one-story, large (but not mansion-sized) house that was built in the '40s. It was decorated "how he was:" elegantly beautiful, not put together by some popular-today-and-gone-tomorrow designer. Cary had the usual large collection of photos and notes from famous people on his walls and tables—but it wasn't overdone. It didn't scream, "Look at me! I'm a big movie star!" It looked more like a wealthy home in Connecticut rather than a Hollywood house. Actually, Cary's house looked a lot like my childhood house and even had the same kind of art deco accents. I was comfortable there.

Cary did have an unusual feature in his bedroom though. Besides the regular accessories like the largest TV you could buy then, he had a custom-made, king-sized bed. It wasn't just any king-sized bed though—lots of people had those. Cary's bed was like a hospital bed, and the feet and head could be raised and lowered. It didn't look like it came from a hospital, but it worked like a patient's bed. An added feature was that each side worked independently, so that one person could be flat and the other could be...however that other person wanted to be. I don't know why he paid what must have been a bundle to have that bed made. He certainly didn't have any physical disabilities. Maybe he just bought it because he could. It was a little strange, but at least his bedroom was tasteful. Not like some other stars' bedrooms I'd seen.

An example of "not tasteful," for instance, was Burt Reynolds' bedroom. Hal Needham (the great stunt man and then movie director) was staying at Burt's house while he was going through a divorce and invited me over one day. He took me on a tour of the house, and eventually we came to the pièce de résistance. (Or so Burt probably thought.) Okay...now there was a bedroom that wasn't even close to tasteful. In fact, it was so tacky it was laughable. The bedroom had way too much glitter on the ceiling. (Sparkly ceilings were all the rage then, but Burt's ceiling made you reach for your sunglasses!) There was so much bright red carpet everywhere that it made the room look like people (a lot of people) had been shot in there.

I couldn't even find the bed at first. There was a huge floor-to-ceiling mirror, and you had to open the side mirrors to find the bed. Of course, in an opened position, those mirrors gave a panoramic view of whatever might be happening in the bed, which was such a huge, four-poster thing, that it looked like another small room was growing inside the bedroom. It sat high off the floor—like a stage. Hal and I were laughing about the "performance" bedroom, and we sat on the bed—which promptly collapsed! Crap! Now what?! We worked for about two hours putting it back together. The stupid bed had been held together by about six nails. So much for "romping" on it. I wondered how that would have worked. (Glad I never found out.)

Cary was not extravagant with his house, and he definitely wasn't extravagant with his money. (*Read* not extravagant *and translate that to* cheap.) I think he married the first 50 cent piece he ever made. He gave me a few gifts, but most of them were kind of strange...and used. I admired two foam pillows that he had so he sent his driver over to my apartment the next day to give them to me. He gave me a gold Dunhill lighter. Not a new one, though—his old one.

One day, Cary had his secretary call me and say, "Mr. Grant thought you'd like some furniture for your house." His driver then arrived with a bed, a round table with leather in the center, a half-round side table, a couple of chairs, and an English settee. Most of the furniture had belonged to Cary's mother—and I still have several of the pieces. They were (are) good pieces...they just weren't exactly the usual jewelry and furs gifts that stars bought their lovers. (Cary was particularly interested in my getting another bed. He knew that Deirdre was staying with me and that she was a lesbian. He didn't think it was right that I had just one bed. Cary, who had roomed with Randolph Scott and Noel Coward, was worried about me and Deirdre? Ever heard of sleeping on the couch, Cary?)

I appreciated his wanting me to have those things, but I was a little irritated when the driver wanted me to sign a receipt because, "Mr. Grant needs this to deduct it off his taxes for a charity contribution." What? Now I was the fucking Salvation Army? Oh well...it was nice stuff, and I already knew he was cheap. (Amazingly, six years later, Cary called and wanted the furniture back! I don't think so! Didn't you already get your tax write-off? Like I said...cheap. Delightful, elegant, suave...and cheap.)

There were other little nice-but-not-new gifts from Cary, as well, like some silver candle holders and a Cheret poster from the Moulin Rouge. He also gave me a small, abstract oil painting by Naomi Lorne and told me it was worth a lot of money. Okay...I still have that ugly thing today, and I'm waiting for the time when it becomes worth "a lot of money." (Near as I can tell, it's worth about $150 today. Not a lot now and not a lot then.)

But one day, Cary did give me something new. He had just returned from shooting on location in Italy, and while I was at his house, he walked me into a spare bedroom that had a huge chifforobe. He threw open the doors, and there were some of the most gorgeous designer clothes I'd ever seen in one spot. He said he'd bought them in Europe as gifts for Bridget Bardot, Ingrid Bergmann, and Sophia Loren (of course), and me. He said I could pick my dress first. Okay, now you're talking my language! I selected an elegant, navy blue, shantung silk, full-length gown with white satin cuffs and a cummerbund. It had small trails of crystals down the sleeves and along the hem. Cary was pleased with my choice and said he'd take me somewhere special in it. (However, when I needed to pay $50 to have the waist taken in, he didn't pop for that. Cheap.)

Cary was sophisticated and fun, and really a great guy to be with. I had been in the Hollywood scene for my entire life, but dating Cary raised my experiences up a notch. I wasn't in love with him, and I don't think he was in love with me either. He saw great genes, a good family, a pretty face, and strong, child-bearing hips...and that's what my appeal really was to him. I knew that, so I also knew that one day, it was going to have to end.

And it did. There was no event: no all-night talks, teary fights, or slamming doors. I just quietly "exited stage left." After a few years of being together, I started giving excuses about why I couldn't see him when he'd call. I was busy working, was on my way to Vegas for another showgirl job, had a kidney stone...whatever. Our love affair just died away. I believe Cary had gotten tired of asking and hearing, "Yes, I did get my period this month," and knew he had to move on to find his baby maker.

I really was busy—but not too busy with work to continue seeing him. My heart was actually what was "busy." I had fallen in love with someone else—the in-demand TV and movie director Don Medford.

Are you thinking, "What? You dropped Cary Grant for...anyone?" Yes, I did...and I still wonder if that was one of the smarter or dumber decisions in my life. Stay with me and see what you think.

SEVEN

The Medford Era

Loretta (Lisa) Malouf (Britton) Mancuso…Now Medford

"How can you marry a guy who's been married four times before and not figure it's going to go bad?" My father was trying to reason with me. He had to get his words in between my crying jags while I was telling him that my marriage to Don Medford was over.

"But, I thought I'd be different," I sobbed.

"You are different, but he's the same jerk who married the other four."

That actually stopped my crying—at least right then, that day. Of course, I knew that I was Don Medford's fifth wife. I had also believed that it would be different with Don and me. I had been taught by my father that "a man's first love is his work, and you don't ever interfere with that. Let him do what he does. Work your life around it." And I had done that. But my father would never have said, "And a man's other love is anybody he can fuck. And he will. Don't think that you'll ever be the only one. There will be lots of 'only ones.'" I didn't learn that second lesson from my father, but Don Medford sure taught it to me.

The end of my Medford Era was a surprise to my parents and to most of my friends. I had never talked about all the problems Don and I had and the extra women in our marriage—not even to my best friend, Gerri Nelson. The end wasn't dramatic. There was no final fight, no big confrontation. One day, about seven years after we were married in Vegas, I just wrote Don a note saying that we were done, and I walked away from everything. There was a lot to walk away from.

Don Medford was a very big man in Hollywood—a highly respected TV and movie director. *You may not know Don Medford unless you're a real TV buff and know more than just "who starred in what." If you're not sure about who he was, I'll fill in some blanks for you.*

Don directed over 300 shows, including episodes for *Baretta, Dr. Kildare, Dynasty, The F.B.I., 12 O'Clock High, The Twilight Zone, The Untouchables, Alfred Hitchcock Presents, The M Squad*—the list just keeps on going! He was known as an "actor's director" because he understood what it took to get a good performance from an actor—any actor—and he got them. (Part of his understanding probably came from having studied acting, and then filmmaking, at Yale School of Drama.) Don's nickname was Midnight Medford because he always worked late. The cast and crew members were delighted because they liked the overtime. The backers were not so thrilled, but Don kept working that way. When I questioned him about this chronic late-night working, he explained, "Sometimes it takes my actors awhile to get into the rhythm of the scene. If I can't get the right performance I want early, then I'll give them more time. At eight o'clock or at midnight—whatever it takes to get the shot." And he did get them—his chase scenes and gun fights were recognized by everyone as the best of the best.

Don thought he was a great judge of acting skills, and he was…at least most of the time. He gave Rod Steiger and James Dean their first acting parts on TV. (Great call on those two, Medford!) Don told me that when Steiger had just started to read for the part, Don said, "Stop. You don't have to say anything. You've got the job." Don could see—hell, anyone could see—that Rod Steiger and James Dean had incredible stage presence; they had the magic.

Don also had some big "misses." He was the same "visionary" who told Paul Newman to get out of acting because he didn't have any talent. Yeah, right. Maybe Paul had done an assignment poorly when they were both at Yale as students and that's what Don remembered. (Whatever made you say that, Medford—you sure blew that one!)

However, to be fair, Newman wasn't so sure about his talent in the beginning either. It was the talk of the town for many years when Paul took out a full-page ad in *Variety* apologizing for his bad acting job in his first film, *Silver Chalice*. By the time I married Don and he told me what he'd said to Paul, Newman had already been nominated for four Oscars for Best Actor. (I asked Don if just maybe he'd been wrong to say that to Newman. No answer from Medford. Surprise.) Good thing that Paul eventually learned how to drive race cars to supplement his income, since know-everything Don Medford thought he couldn't act!

Don also kept turning down Cher when she'd ask him to cast her in one of his shows. He never would, and when I asked him why not, he said, "She just can't act. She's a singer." (Okay, Medford. Did you plan to mention that to the Academy when they gave her the Oscar for Best Actress?)

I met Don in 1961 when I auditioned for some TV show that he was directing. He asked me out during the filming, and even though I was dating Cary Grant at the time, I went that first time…and kept on dating him. (I knew that my time with Cary was not going to be "forever" unless I turned into a baby maker, so…why not?)

Don took me to the Fog Cutter for dinner on our first date. I should have known then that he was screwed up. All the way there and back, he'd drive through every red light and stop for the green ones. I pointed this out to him and he said, "I can't be bothered with trivia."

Okay, that was strange. I found out later that when he was working, he was definitely "bothered with trivia." Everything had to be perfect—the lighting, the camera angles, the costumes, the actors' makeup, the way they said every line—all the "trivia" had to be just the way he wanted it. It was the details in his life that Don couldn't be bothered with. Like… you aren't supposed to be fucking every woman that moves when you're married!

Don was tough to turn down. He was not only a powerful Hollywood director, but he was also a real hunk. He was 6'4", with a big chest, long muscular legs, blue eyes, and a big dick. (It just doesn't get much better than that.) He was well educated (two master's degrees, including one in chemical engineering) and had flown B17 bombers in the War. He was also 20 years older than I was when I met him, but what did I care?

I let "Cary and Lisa" fade away when I realized that I'd fallen in love with Don and believed that he was "The One." We got married in Vegas after I'd worked my second show at the Dunes, in 1964. (It's telling that I didn't even write,

"Got married today," or anything else wedding related in my calendar. My neglecting to do that should have told me something.) Don wanted to get married right away because his parents were coming to visit him from Florida, and he didn't want me in our house without our being married. He had a strange sense of morality.

The exact wedding date wasn't all that memorable, but I do remember the pink wool knit suit I wore with the matching hat, both of which were trimmed in sable. I also remember my ring, which was more unforgettable than the ceremony. It looked like a golf ball and had 42 diamonds. Just the right size for an important director's wife! Don gave me another ring that night that had 25 rubies shaped into a flower with diamonds at the center. Nice! (Both of the rings were stolen when my apartment in L.A. was broken into years later. Easy come, easy...)

I thought it was pretty funny in April of 1965 when Walter Winchell reported in his "Man About Town" column in the *Los Angeles Herald Examiner* that Don and I were getting married. He wrote: "Movietown's Don Medford and his (current) wife are having their marriage Mexi-cancelled. His next bride will be Lisa Britton, former Vegas show girl." Just goes to show that you can't trust what you read about celebrities now, and you couldn't trust it then. We'd already been married for over six months. At least I thought we were.

When I was signing divorce papers about seven years later, Don's lawyer said he didn't know why he was bothering to file the papers. He told me that he wasn't sure that our marriage was even legal since Don hadn't had his other marriage Mexi-cancelled when we eloped. Just great! Add *bigamist* to the words that describe Don Medford!

But while Don and I were married, a new Hollywood opened up to me. It wasn't the Hollywood of my growing-up years or the Hollywood of my acting career, where I was way too often just one of the smaller players. It wasn't even the Hollywood I knew with Cary Grant because we didn't do that much flashy Hollywood life together. This was a different level of "belonging in Hollywood"—Don Medford was an important director, and he was rich.

Don and I went out to dinner and partied at the homes of serious movie stars, directors, and producers. Of course, I wore sable and mink and lots of diamonds on those occasions. I certainly couldn't let anyone think that Don Medford was cheap! And he was not...he did enjoy spreading his cash around. He loved to spend money on me, and he regularly came home with over-the-top gifts. His money went to buy me beautiful things—and to hookers and the horses. Most of Don's free time, and a bunch of his "disposable cash," were disposed of at the races.

Some of our closest friends were Richard Alan and Emily Simmons. (Richard was the Emmy-nominated writer of *The Price of Tomatoes* for the *Dick Powell Theatre*.) We had lots of fun times with Stirling and Margo Siliphant too. Stirling had created the TV series *Route 66* and wrote the screenplay, and also received an Oscar for *In the Heat of the Night*. Don especially liked to hang around with writers, particularly for dinner parties at our house or theirs, because they were passionate and imaginative and funny.

We'd often go to Dean and Jeanne Martin's house for dinner too. Their house in Beverly Hills was really gorgeous, with the most beautiful green carpets I'd ever seen. Dean was as lovely as his house…but his wife Jeanne? That was a different story. Although Dean's stage image was a hard-drinking womanizer, it was Jeanne who was the "bad guy," and not on stage—in real life! The "adoring and devoted wife" image that she tried to portray publically didn't surface when there wasn't an audience. Don and I didn't count as "audience" because we were friends, and neither of us was likely to break into applause just because she pretended to be the perfect wife. We'd show up for dinner, and then we'd all watch a movie together. Well, not all of us. Jeanne would duck out as soon as the movie started. She couldn't be bothered to hang around us or Dean with the lights down low.

My "friendship" with Jeanne Martin cooled to an ice cube when she wanted me to testify against Dean at their divorce hearing. I got a call from Dorothy Lamour's son telling me that Jeanne wanted me to swear in court that Dean fooled around on her in Vegas. (I don't know why Dorothy's son made that call. Maybe he was her lawyer?) I told him to tell Jeanne that I would not say that because I had never seen Dean sleep around, and she could just go fuck herself with that bullshit request. My response to her request didn't strengthen our friendship.

But Dean—he was a sweetheart. I counted Dean Martin among my friends until the day he died. I still think of Dean as "the loveliest man in America" and remember his cute stories. I can hear him telling me about his "ugly nose" when he was growing up. (I could relate to ugly nose stories.) Dean said that he was a "duffus" in school, with a really crappy-looking nose. He said he had a huge schoolboy crush on a girl named Betty who wouldn't give him a second look. In fact, not even a good first look. When he was appearing at the Sands, old schoolmate Betty showed up backstage. Dean said he was really nice to her because he was so pleased with what he saw. "So here's Betty, with her stringy hair and her ugly, big ass and loser husband, and now I'm 'Dean Martin'. Sweet justice!"

Don and I also went to a Warner Brothers party where I learned a valuable life-long lesson. Julie Newmar was there looking staggeringly beautiful, except for her feet, which were the size of Belgian waffles. About halfway through the party, she slowly walked out on the pool's diving board—stark naked—and dove in. There was complete silence while everyone thought about what they'd just seen and relived the image of that gorgeous body.

Then Delores Del Rio, who was in her 50s at the time, took off all her clothes, walked out on the board, and dove in right after Julie. I couldn't believe my eyes! She was even more beautiful than Julie Newmar! After her dive, I went inside a cabana where Delores was drying off and wearing a white turban towel. She looked incredibly "old-Hollywood glamorous!"

I asked her, "How do you stay so beautiful? Where did you get the confidence to follow Julie Newmar like that?"

Her answer was immediate. "Sleep…sleep…sleep….it's a women's best friend. A woman needs at least eight hours of sleep every night. And stay calm and peaceful. Don't remember tomorrow what you were mad about today." I thought about that on our drive home and vowed to "not remember tomorrow what I was mad about today." That advice has served me pretty well—although it certainly extended the amount of time that I put up with Don's crap.

Not all my partying fun during our marriage, however, was with or because of Don Medford. I did have friends that were "Lisa's," not "Don Medford's wife's." I remember stopping by comedian Dick Martin's house on Doheny Drive in Hollywood Hills. Although Dick and I had been friends for years, going back to my early Vegas days, I didn't usually just drop in on him. That wasn't a smart thing to do when you didn't know just what craziness might be going on. But something compelled me to stop one day. I knew Dick was home because I saw his cars in the driveway.

After I rang the bell a few times, Dick came to the door, stark naked except for a silk top hat. He was holding a trumpet and had a hard-on. "Lisa! Come on in! Join the party!" This was right about noon! I passed on that party, but I still wonder just what was going on there during a sunny, ordinary weekday in L.A.!

Near the end of the Medford Era, I certainly had to find my own fun. In 1969, while I was still legally married to Don (but just barely), I was back and forth from our house to living in my own apartment again. Every Sunday at 10:00 a.m., Sammy Kahn (the songwriter) would host a brunch at his house. It was a casual get-together with movie people and musicians for great food, a swim in his pool, and lots of laughing. I went there a couple Sundays a month just to schmooze and socialize.

One day, Kahn said, "Someone wants to meet to you," and handed me the phone. It was Warren Beatty. We talked nice for about 20 minutes and that was it...at least for me. I never really liked to date actors—they were too much about themselves. Five days later however, Beatty called me up at midnight. How rude was that?

Warren said, "How about if you leave your door open and I'll come in and fuck you? I don't know what you look like, so it'll be really sexy."

"No thanks. It won't be sexy. I know what you look like," I said, and hung up. In the next few weeks, Warren called several more times with the same question, and I always gave him the same response.

Sometime later, I was at a party at Sharon Tate's house, two weeks before she was murdered. Who was there? Warren Beatty. I sneaked up behind him and whispered in his ear, "How about leaving your door open and I'll come over and fuck you? I don't know what you look like, so it'll be really sexy." Without turning around, he hollered "Lisa Medford!" We had a good laugh...but I never left the door open, and he never came over.

While we were together, Don and I lived in great apartments in L.A, but we never owned a house in California. Don hated owning things. He thought it was "bourgeoisie" to own a house. I think home ownership was just too "permanent" for him. Like everybody else we knew, we rented a beach house in Malibu while we kept our apartment in Beverly Hills. Jason Robards and Lauren Bacall lived just north of us on the beach. About twice a month, about three or four o'clock in the afternoon, Robards would come staggering up the beach—plastered. He knew he couldn't make it all the way home, and he was still sober enough to know there'd be hell to pay when he got there, so he'd stop off at our house. He never knocked. He'd just climb up the back stairs and wander around until he found Don. After they'd talk for awhile, Robards always wanted "just a little nap." No food, nothing to drink...just sleep, and he'd sack out on the couch.

Pretty soon the phone would ring, and it would be Lauren Bacall. I don't know how she got our number (because we'd never actually met) or how she always knew Jason would be there. I think she had Robards-radar. I'd answer the phone and hear, with that can-only-be-Lauren-Bacall voice, "Hey, Lisa. This is Betty. Is that cocksucker sleeping on your couch again? If he is, get his sorry ass home. And don't let Don drive him. Make the bastard walk."

Don and I would look over at Jason, whose eyes were now half opened because he knew what was coming, and tell him, "It's time, Jason." Don would drive him home and drop him off about a block away. We sure couldn't let him walk—who knew where he'd end up?

The on-location times with Don were even better than the parties. I have some stand-out memories of going with him to watch him work, and to do whatever he needed me to do. One of those times, when he needed to call on Lisa's "little extra" that she brought to the job, was when we were in San Francisco while Don was shooting *The Organization* with Sidney Poitier starring as Virgil Tibbs.

One Saturday night at dinner, a crown suddenly popped off one of Sidney's teeth. He was not a happy camper since that meant the end of his great steak dinner and a quick trip to the dentist. Don wasn't happy either because he immediately worried that he might have to change some camera angles to avoid the missing crown until Sidney could get it fixed. But the crown had been on a back tooth, and Don decided that it wouldn't interfere with his work, so…at least Don was able to enjoy the rest of his dinner. Low on empathy, high on work focus.

Don got a lot more interested in finding a dentist the next morning when he woke up with a horrible toothache! Great—it's a Sunday morning! It's always a Sunday when you need a dentist. The good thing was that if you're Sidney Poitier and Don Medford, you can get a dentist to show up just about any day or time. Calls were made and they had their dentist ready and waiting. When the dentist examined Don's tooth, he said he needed a root canal, but the dentist didn't want to do it without his dental assistant.

Don said, "That's okay. My wife will do it. She can do anything." (I wish he would have remembered that when I wanted parts in his TV shows. But, I put on the smock and a mask, and I became Lisa Medford, dental assistant.)

The dentist (and Lisa, dental assistant) got Don set up with the novocaine, and then we went to Sidney's room to start him. Sidney wasn't in the chair yet; he was pacing around, checking the missing crown in the mirror. When he saw me walk in with the dentist in my cute white smock and mask, he started laughing so hard, he lay down on the floor. Sidney thought that was just about the funniest thing he'd seen. His director's wife was now going to work on his teeth! "So, Lisa, did Don finally give you a part?" Sidney still laughs about that when he sees me and tells people, "Hey, this is my dentist!"

Another time on location, Don's lack of concern about "trivia" almost got us killed. Don was directing *The Hunting Party* in Spain starring Candice Bergen, Gene Hackman, Mitch Ryan, and Oliver Reed. Naturally, I went along—who'd pass up a trip to Spain? Just as naturally, so did Gerri Nelson and my sister Joey. (Gerri went with Don and me almost everywhere, and I took my sister when she was available.)

On location in Spain with Oliver Reed, Candice Bergen
and Don Medford

For part of the filming, we needed to fly from Madrid to
Almeria, and the production company had chartered a real
wreck of a plane to fly us there. The producers were over budget on the film, and they didn't pop for a "luxury airliner."
Don didn't care about the plane—that was trivia. He was
comfortable in any kind of plane. He figured that since he'd
lived flying those bombers in the war, no other plane was going
to raise his blood pressure.

Don and I were sitting in the front of the plane with Gerri
and Joey, and Oliver Reed (drunk as usual) and the rest of the
cast were sitting behind us. Before we took off, I had pushed
aside the little curtain covering the window and could see oil
coming out of the engine. That just didn't seem right.

I tried to warn Don that I could see oil where oil should not be, but he was already going to sleep and told me, "Just don't look out the window." Don then reached over me, looked out the window, and said, "Yeah, you're right. We're going to crash." He closed my curtain and went to sleep.

When the engines fired up, Don didn't even open his eyes. "Yep," I told him. "We're going to crash." Nothing out of Medford.

Okay, we made it to Almeria, and the pilot told us to put on our seat belts, put out our cigarettes, and get ready to land. I started sniffing. "Hey, Don!" I yelled. Wake up! I can smell smoke. The plane's on fire!"

Now Don was pissed off at me because I woke him up again. "It's just cigarettes, Lisa. Leave me alone." No, it wasn't cigarettes—that was the smell of wires burning. We were coming down, down, down, getting ready to land, and I looked toward Don's side of the plane just in time to see a huge flame streak out of the engine and sweep toward the back of the plane.

"Okay, open up your damn eyes now! There's fire!" Don finally stirred himself as we landed and as another huge fire bolt raced down the side of the plane. Suddenly, everybody wanted to get off that plane! I think even Oliver sobered up! As soon as the plane landed and stopped, we jumped out of the non-burning side and could see the engine barely attached to the plane hanging just off the ground.

Through that whole episode, I wasn't afraid of dying. I was just so glad that I was right and that I could say, "I told you so!" I repeated that to Don several times while I also ragged on him because, "My sister and Gerri were in that plane! We all could have been killed in that crappy plane!"

We probably should have commended the pilot for an incredible landing "under fire," but I don't know if he even realized it. I think he was drunk too.

During *The Hunting Party* shoot, poor Mitch Ryan did it again. He just kept getting drunk when he was supposed to be working. He'd already gotten fired from *Dark Shadows* in 1967 for showing up drunk, and here he was again...every morning...totally lit up. He knew it wasn't going well for him on the *The Hunting Party* set, and Don had been all over his ass about the booze.

One day, I'd gone to Morocco to do some shopping and came back with presents. (No hash though. The camera crew was not happy with me when they found out I didn't have hash. They knew what presents they considered quality.) Anyway, I'd bought a really fun Moroccan tunic for Don. Unfortunately, he wasn't thrilled with it, and he suggested I give it to Mitch Ryan who probably needed some cheering up. So I did, and I had a long talk with Mitch about trying to stay off the bottle just long enough to make it through the filming. The movie was close to wrapping, for God's sake! Unfortunately, a week later, Don fired him. Mitch didn't have many scenes left and James Stacy was hired to replace him.

Soon after Mitch left, Don and Gene Hackman got into it. There was a scene where Gene was supposed to be shot nude from the back. You wouldn't see his whole butt (this was 1970!), but enough that Don needed him to be nude. The "back nudity" had been written into Gene's contract, and he'd agreed to it. The problem was, when it came time to shoot the scene, Hackman balked. Don was pissed and hollered, "What do you mean you won't do it?! You signed a contract that said you would. Don't you have any goddamn integrity?"

Hackman's reply was, "Why are you talking about integrity when your wife is fucking Mitch Ryan? Or is that why you canned him?" Don hit Hackman, and down he went. Thank God his nose wasn't broken—there were more scenes to shoot!

Supporting Don's work meant that I did whatever he asked of me when I was with him while he worked. One day, Don was scouting a location in the Vasquez Rocks in northern L.A. County. We were standing high on a cliff while we were waiting for his stunt man to show up. To get a better eye on what he'd shoot, Don was scanning the drop down the cliff and the horizon with a small film viewer. I was in my standard uniform of the time: a pair of jeans and a t-shirt with my hair down, long and loose.

"Hey, Lisa, can you just roll down that hill?" Don asked.

"Where? You don't mean this hill, do you?" That was a damn big hill, and it had rocks and weeds and shit all over it!

"Yeah, this one right here."

Good wife that I was, I said, "Okay," dropped down, and rolled all the way down the hill. While I was climbing back up, picking rocks, twigs, and pieces of glass out of my hair and my butt, the stunt man appeared.

Don said to him, "Good. I'm glad you're here. I think this is the spot. Let's try a roll." The stunt guy started clearing out the debris along the path he was going to roll down.

"Hey, wait a damn minute! What are you doing?" I wanted to know.

The stunt man replied, "Well, I'm sure not going to roll over rocks!" Thanks, Don! He never told me that it was okay to clear out the path first. Oh well...

Supporting Don also meant that I did whatever I could to make sure that he had what he wanted—and Don wanted a lot! He was a grown-up kid. He was all appetite, bouncing around from toy to toy. I was 20 years younger, but I was the parent when it came to looking ahead and trying to plan a life together. I had heard enough of his whining about not having the money to buy the movie rights for his own property. (Of course, he didn't have enough because as soon as it came in, it was spent on another toy. The $1,400 a month he paid in child support for his daughter didn't help either. But still, Don made a lot of money. He sure should have been able to buy whatever movie rights he wanted!)

But because I wanted to make my husband happy, I began to save and save and save. He gave me a down payment to have a sable coat made. I already had three mink coats, but that was how Don operated—minks were great, but sable was even better. Instead of ordering the coat, I ran to the bank with the money and opened an account with his name only. (Boy, I was really stupid back then.) I left the bank with the signature card to "get him to sign it" and then went right back into the bank with his forged signature. Whenever I'd get my hands on some more cash, it went right into that savings account. Don kept asking me when the sable was going to be done, and I'd put him off with excuses. I'd tell him that the fur pieces didn't match or the lapel was lumpy. I just made up reasons to stall him. It didn't take long for me to squirrel away a little over $10,000.

After rat holing cash for awhile, Don told me he'd read a book he really liked and we flew to Texas to meet the writer, Larry McMurtry. All the way home, he whined about not having enough money to buy the script.

"So, how much do you need?" I asked.

"About 10 grand for the deposit—a lot more than I can put my hands on in cash." I didn't respond to Don's answer. I just smiled and felt like the best wife ever.

I got the money from the savings account and handed it over, telling him that now he could buy his first script. I just knew that Don Medford was going to be indebted to and love me forever! Nope. He spent his (my!) $10,000 to take some hooker to the Orient. He blew all the money on the trip and never bought the script or made the movie. That movie was *The Last Picture Show.* Peter Bogdanovich directed the picture, and it won two Oscars, had 14 more movie award wins, and received 16 more nominations!

Doesn't that stupid Medford remind you of John Edwards and Bill Clinton and Eliot Spitzer and all those other sleazeball guys who screwed their careers just for a piece of ass? Sure they recovered (somewhat) and so did Don Medford. But if he had bought The Last Picture Show, *I wouldn't have to explain to you who Don Medford was! You would have known, just like when someone says* Spielberg *or* Scorsese *or…*Peter Bogdanovich. *Don Medford…dumb shit.*

Did the "take the money and run to the Orient" trick cause me to leave Don? It probably should have, but it didn't. I continued to work hard to believe that he was "just under so much pressure from work" that he did stupid things like that and that he really loved only me. And I'm sure he did love me, but in a lot of ways, sex addiction is like drug addiction—a hard habit to break once it grabs hold of you.

I didn't only have great times when I was on location with Don, though...I had my own on-location good times with my new friends, Steve McQueen and Suzanne Pleshette.

Just Lisa's Fun...and Steve McQueen's

My agent, Fred, sent me to Western Town at Paramount Studios where the filming for *Nevada Smith* had already started. I met with Steve McQueen and Henry Hathaway, the director. Whatever I said or whatever he saw in me, Steve McQueen said, "Let's hire her to be a Cajun girl." Great! The good news and the bad news was that the filming was moving to location in Louisiana. Under regular circumstances, this could have been okay, but Hurricane Betsy had just wrecked that state, which wasn't so okay.

I got on a plane two days after meeting with Steve and Henry, along with Suzanne Pleshette and some of the other actors, and we flew to New Orleans. We could see floating dead animals from the plane windows. It was so gross! The storm had blown the windows out of the bungalows at our hotel (which was somewhere near Lake Charles), and they had put up temporary coverings just to try to keep the mosquitoes out. Sure—keep about a billion mosquitoes out of your room? That wasn't going to happen, so they had those swirly, stinky mosquito smoker things all over the rooms. I think those damn bugs ate that smoky shit for dinner!

Even though Suzanne was one of the stars, we roomed together for the first week because the hotel had run out of usable rooms. I think our bungalow should have made the list of "unusable," but it was what it was. Two things that I found out about Suzanne right away were that she never complained and that she talked even dirtier than I did!

The hotel was bad, but the working conditions were even more miserable. There was black, swampy shit all over everything, and it didn't help that many of the scenes were right out there in the swamp. Smelly, wet, ugly swamp shit, every day. At night, we'd just take off our clothes right outside our doors and leave them out there for the wardrobe people to collect. We didn't need to bring that swamp smell inside our room!

The working conditions were bad and so was my part. During one scene, we were working in the swamp (picking rice, I think), and we were supposed to be soaking wet. You'd think that with almost 100 percent humidity a wet shirt would have been a "given." But it took Hathaway so long to set up the shot that my shirt would dry off. Then they'd water me down again with a spray bottle to get my blouse to cling to me. Then it would dry, and they'd water me again. This went on too many times. Finally Hathaway hollered to the wardrobe guy, "If I had known her tits were so big, we'd have gotten a bigger bottle! Find a hose or something. Get her wet and keep her that way!"

Another day, Suzanne and I and some others were back in the damn rice field. I was supposed to look up at the camera twice during the scene, and that's what I did. Hathaway (who hollered all the time) started yelling at me. At first, I wasn't even sure that he was yelling at me, even though I was only about 12 feet away from him He was real indiscriminate in his yelling.

Finally he said, "You, with the big tits. Quit looking up so much." Okay, we did the scene again, and I looked up twice like I'd been told to do.

"Cut," Hathaway yelled again, "Are you stupid?" What? Am I in trouble again? Enough, already! I tried to pull my feet out of the mud, but one of my tennis shoes stayed on and the other was buried in the gunk. I didn't care. I held up my skirt and limped over to him with one shoe on.

Everybody knew that Hathaway had had a colostomy. "Listen," I whispered to him. "Everybody knows that you shit in a bag, but just because you haven't had a good dump in 20 years, it's not fair to take it out on me! Quit yelling at me. I'm only looking up twice, like I'm supposed to!"

Hathaway stared at me for a long time and then started laughing. We shot the scene again, I looked up twice, and he didn't yell.

Of course, I think he may have gotten his revenge later. Almost all the scenes that I was in ended up on the cutting room floor, and I'm not even listed in the credits on IMDb for *Nevada Smith*. Fine, I don't care. I know I was in it, I have the photos. And besides that, I was Don Medford's wife. (And I still get the residual checks, so screw you, Henry Hathaway.)

That shooting was full of ugly stuff. One day we were in the rice fields (again!) when I looked down and saw a snake curled up by my feet about two feet away from me, in about four feet of water! It was a big-ass diamondback water snake.

(I recognized it from the pictures that our hotel had handed out of "Things to Beware Of." Nice place.) I was working hard at staying calm, but damn...that was a big snake!

Suzanne Pleshette and the "Swamp Queen"
Lisa on location for *Nevada Smith*

I said to one of the nearby extras who was playing a guard and who could also see the snake, "Don't say anything. If Suzanne sees this, she'll just panic…she's afraid of every damn thing."

I stood perfectly still until the extra came back with seven guys who looked so scared I knew they wouldn't be much help. One of them slowly and carefully handed me a sickle. Handed it to me! I whispered to the "guards," "Shoot the damn thing! Don't any of those guns work"? The answer was that they were only prop guns. Great, I had no choice. I wasn't going to be one of those pansy-asses; I had to go after that snake with the sickle.

I remember thinking, "What if this is a prop sickle and it breaks? What if the snake bites me? Well…at least I'll be in all the papers, and that'll be good publicity." I took a mighty swing at it, cut right through the coiled part, and the snake fell apart in pieces! Everyone knew what was happening by then, and Steve was hollering, "She did it! She killed the snake…she killed the snake!" I was that day's hero.

A year later, Don was in a pre-production meeting with Steve and his people to discuss the possibility of Don directing *Bullet*. When Don came back from the meeting, he told me that McQueen had said, "Hey, wait a minute. Don Medford. Aren't you Lisa Medford's husband?"

When Don said that he was, Steve jumped and shouted, "Damn! Your wife has balls! She cut a huge snake into pieces!" Don was blown away because I'd never told him the story. He also wasn't very happy. He didn't like being known as "Lisa Medford's husband." He turned down the chase-directing job because he'd signed to do part three of *Planet of the Apes*. I tried to talk Don into working on *Bullet,* but he kept protesting that it would violate his "integrity" to back out of the other film.

My response was less than you'd expect from a "loving, devoted wife," but perfectly appropriate, I thought! "Integrity? What integrity? You've been married five times, and you still screw everything walking! So much for your word!"

As it worked out, Don didn't get to direct *Bullet* or *Planet of the Apes, Part Three.* The third in the monkey movies was delayed for two years, and someone else directed it. So there ya go— another great opportunity for Don down the toilet. Oh well...

The shooting of *Nevada Smith* wasn't one of the greatest times I'd ever had, but the after-hours time made up for the hot, sweaty, getting-yelled-at filming time. There was almost nowhere to go around our location that met our criteria for fun—that hadn't gotten wrecked by Betsy—so Steve, Suzanne, and I made our own good times. Every once in a while, we'd just hang out and watch TV, but more often we'd go to the local drive-in theater or one of the local, crappy bars.

The first time we went to the local drive-in was almost our last. We were in a convertible, and Steve and Suzanne were smoking grass like crazy. I didn't like that shit because it gave me a monster headache, but since I was sitting between them, I was getting a "killer contact high." We were watching *Beach Blanket Bingo* when the ads for the concession stand came on: "Go to the Concession Stand. It's Time for a Snack!" There were all these picture of pizza and hot dogs and all the stuff we were not getting from the movie's Commissary during the day. (I was accustomed to better food from the on-location movie commissaries when I was shooting a film. Guess Betsy blew away all the decent cooking stuff and left us with crap like "greens" and crawfish (with their damn heads still on!) and shitty, too-local food. New Orleans famous cuisine it was not!)

Steve leaned over me to say, "Come on, Suzanne. Go get our food! I can't go in there…I'm a fucking star! People are going to mob me! You go!"

Suzanne reared up. "I'm just as big a star as you are! You go!" They stared at each other for a minute, and then both of them looked at me. Okay, I sure couldn't say that I was as big a star as either one of them. Fine, I can be Lisa Medford— drive-in catering service.

I took Steve's $50 to the concession stand and spent it all! We ate, and ate, and ate. We weren't even watching the movie anymore—we just worked on eating all the food! As we were finishing up, it started to rain, and when we looked around, everyone else was gone! We could see some guy walking toward us in the rain. He was probably going to tell us that the movie was over and we had to get out of there. And we did! We roared out of that drive-in as fast as we could and went careening down the mud-slick road.

Steve was driving, driving, driving—we had no idea where the hell we were. We found out when we got stuck in the mud and got out. We were stuck in a damn cemetery! I don't even remember how we got out of there. I just remember Suzanne and me pushing the car, and Steve being no help at all because he was totally freaked out about being in a cemetery. Suzanne and I never let him live that one down.

Once in awhile, a bunch of us would go to a "real" restaurant that really was not too good. The famous New Orleans cuisine had gotten blown away in the hurricane. One night, Bill Holden, Richard Widmark, and some blonde were at the restaurant at a different table when we arrived. There were eight of us, and they had a table with three people. The great actor, Arthur Kennedy, was with us and went over to talk to Holden. He came back and said that Holden would like us to join them.

Steve said that Holden, Widmark, and the blonde should sit with us. We had a bigger table, and we could pull up more chairs. However, Bill Holden told Arthur, "I'm a bigger star than he is. He should come to my table."

Steve's response was, "No thanks. Tell him that he can go fuck himself." That ended the skirmish, and Holden's party came to our table.

I ended up with Richard Widmark on my right and Arthur Kennedy on my left. During the dinner, Widmark turned in his seat and had his back to me to talk to someone else. Arthur (gentleman that he was) said, "Don't turn your back to the lady. That's rude."

Widmark's reply was even more rude. "I don't have to sit around and talk to some stupid cunt." I took my fork and stabbed him in the leg. That took care of that dinner party— our group got up and left.

It wasn't party time every night though. Sometimes it was just go to work, go to the bungalow, go to bed. One boring night, I was sound asleep when the phone rang. It was Steve. "Lisa, you've got to come to my bungalow right away. Don't let anyone see you. Hurry up...this is terrible!"

I threw on some shorts and raced over there. Steve flung open the door and was standing there totally naked, holding his arms away from his body. "Look—it's horrible! What is this shit?" he yelled.

Steve was completely covered in red dots! They were everywhere—his arms, chest, all over his legs, and his dick! "Not good, Steve! Let me see your tongue. Maybe you have the measles? We should get the doctor."

He was horrified! "Measles! Then they'll quarantine us, and we'll be stuck in this hellhole for weeks! Don't call the doctor!"

"Well, maybe it's not measles," I suggested. "Did you ever have measles?"

"Hell, I don't know!"

"Well, didn't your mother ever tell you if you did?" I asked.

"My mother didn't tell me shit! She was a fucking whore!" Steve yelled.

After Steve gave in to my "we-need-the-doctor" insistence, I called and the set doctor came right over. (For me, he would have asked, "Why are you calling me in the middle of the night?" For Steve McQueen, he got his ass there pronto.) The doctor said they were flea bites. After the shoot, Steve had jumped into his pool (he had a lot nicer bungalow than I did), and when he got out and fell asleep, the damn fleas attacked him!

When I found out it wasn't serious, I started laughing. Steve McQueen looked really funny standing there with his red-dotted dick. He looked down and started laughing with me, and the doctor figured we'd gone nuts. The doctor left to find some lotion—giving us you-two-are-really-strange looks all the way out the door.

When I finally got home, I was telling Don about all the good times I'd had with Steve and Suzanne and told him how happy I was that Suzanne was my new friend.

"You don't want to make friends with Suzanne. She's an actress—a real actress. Not like you. She'll go in and do an acting job on her way to her mother's funeral. As soon as anything in your friendship interferes in the slightest way with her career, you're out. No one is as important as an actor's career. Stay away from the real actors."

Don was definitely raining on my parade. We had already been married long enough for me to know what he was saying was, "No one is as important as my career." His warning to me didn't necessarily apply to Suzanne (he was wrong…we did remain friends) but it did apply to Don Medford. He didn't want to be married to anyone who could potentially interfere with anything he wanted to do in his work or personal life. He didn't want to be married to an actress.

Winding Down: The End of the Medford Era

It's sad that what should have been an exciting milestone for Don and me actually contributed to the end for us.

We had finally bought a house together in Vegas. The reason we purchased it probably wasn't all that great—or based on any kind of truth, now that I think about it. Don told me that the IRS was after his money and we needed to set up a residency in Vegas to avoid taxes. (What did I know? Like they wouldn't find him in Vegas?) We bought a home on the Tropicana Golf Course for $60,000. (I remember that the payments were $478 a month.)

Our house had some great things going for it, like the huge windows that looked out to the pool. The unusual part was that the living room wall with the arched windows came across one end of the pool, and you could swim right from the outside pool into the house by going under the windows. Very cool. But the house had some have-to-go things too— like the cheap white shag carpeting that looked like a dead poodle—a really big dead poodle. It was all over the huge front entry and down the two stairs that went into the living room. That really needed to come out of there! We replaced all of it with Mexican octagonal tile that we had custom dyed in a rich burnt umber color. (Many years later, before it was torn down to make a casino parking lot, I saw the inside of the house one last time. Someone had removed all that gorgeous (and expensive!) tile and replaced it with white linoleum with gold fleurs-de-lis. Can you believe it? Well, money never guaranteed good taste!)

Speaking of no guarantee of good taste—one of the really questionable touches in the house when we purchased it was a large mannequin pis statue—that little boy who is pissing water. I sure wasn't too keen on it, but it was real handy for filling my plant-watering can.

Betty Grable was our next door neighbor with about 30 feet in between the sides of our houses. One day she suggested that we should plant a hedge between the houses because our yards weren't fenced in. We decided on oleander bushes, and she planted 15 white ones and I put in 15 pink ones. Those things were 20 feet high the last time I saw the house!

One weekend, Don didn't show up after he'd promised to help me work on the new brick floor in the game room. Okay, he missed that weekend...but then he didn't show for the second weekend in a row. That was it! I drove to L.A and didn't find Don at home, but I did find a pile of mail. In it was a confirmation from the William Morris Agency for the weekend for Mr. and Mrs. Medford at Shelter Island. But I wasn't going to Shelter Island. Okay, I knew what was going on, and once again, I was getting screwed over by Medford. I just went back to Vegas and connected with Ladi—who was waiting for me at the Frontier. (*Remember Ladi—the wonderful musician who was at the Frontier with the Karel Gott show? He was there when I was fired for beating up the guard. Still having a problem? Okay, you can go back to Chapter Three and get a little refresher.*)

This "Shelter Island" ugliness was a part of the infamous 1968 that I've been mentioning. Medford had showed his ass for the last time with me, and I was in love with Ladi. It was time to follow my heart...to Europe, where Ladi was going. But first, I had to do something about that house—the place that was going to be the dream home for Don and me, but that had turned into a nightmare.

Fate intervened right after that horrible Shelter Island fiasco. One day there was a knock on the door and a nice-looking man was standing there. He asked if he could look at the house. Sure. (That was during a time when you'd let strangers in). He walked all around, didn't say much, and then asked me if it was for sale. Well, no...not yet at least. He asked if I'd sell it for $160,000 and if I'd carry the second mortgage.

SOLD—to Steve Wynn! (Yes, **the** Steve Wynn, who was "just" Steve Wynn at the time.) I remember that his payments were $1,248 a month, and he paid them on time every month. He later sold the house to Paul Anka who then sold it to the Riviera. The last time I heard about it, the asking price was $5.3 million—with linoleum in the living room! Eventually the house was razed so there could be yet another parking lot on the Strip.

I didn't push the idea of a divorce with Medford. I didn't care about that. I certainly had no intention of getting married again! And I never did. It was actually a few years before we were divorced, and Don initiated it. He had wife number six waiting in the wings. And after that, there was number seven and then number eight. Some people ought not to be given marriage licenses over and over and over again. They obviously can't get it right—so they should just be barred from doing it again.

I asked Don where he found his last wife, Lynn Parker—a real loser! He told me he met her when she was knocking on cars in the parking lot of the Barbary Coast offering $20 blow-jobs. Oh, now that's a real sign of a great wife! Don always did like a woman who was a go-getter.

I don't know where Don is now. He just seemed to disappear several years ago, and no one could find him—not the hotel where he'd being living, not his kids, not his friends—no one knew where he was. I was worried that Parker had killed him and filed a Missing Persons Report with the Sheriff's Department. They got back to me with the news that he wasn't dead, but that his wife didn't want any information given out to anyone. About a year later, I found out that he was in the Motion Picture Country Home for awhile, which housed ailing movie people. I went to see him a few times, but he was very ill and very unhappy.

I remember the last thing that Don said to me. "Of all the women I married, you were my only wife." That was a sad day for both of us.

But today, I don't know if he's still there, or if he's dead or alive. I always knew that Don was so ornery that when Death came calling, he'd bite him in the ass and send him packing. But I don't know how long he was able to keep up that attitude.

So, although I don't know now what eventually happened to Don, at least in 1968, I knew what I wanted to happen for me. I wanted a new life that included Ladi Staidl. Along with my acting, and modeling and marrying, and un-marrying, I had followed my showgirl heart and continued to work Vegas. But now, I wanted to give up being a showgirl. I had lost the spirit that drove me to the Vegas applause. I couldn't hear it any more. It was time to move on.

My "Schroeder," Ladi Staidl

Ladislav "Schroeder" Staidl

"I think that you're my Schroeder," I told Ladi while he was at the piano doing what he did so well, and all the time. He was playing one of his own compositions.

He crinkled his nose and asked, "What is Schroeder?"

I handed him the newspaper with the Charlie Brown cartoon, and he read it very, very slowly—there was that issue of "English, not so great."

Ladi finally looked up and grinned. "Yes, I am Schroeder playing piano and you are Lucy. You have a hair of curls and big mouth like Lucy!" Those became our pet names for each other: Schroeder and Lucy, especially during the times in Vegas and in Europe when I'd spend wonderful, peaceful hours just listening to his music.

After that Shelter Island incident with Medford and my walk-away from the Vegas showgirl life, I knew I had to get my head and my heart straight and that it would mean getting out of everywhere that was too familiar to me. L.A. was tainted because Don and his girlfriends were there, and Vegas reminded me of Ladi, and he had gone back to Prague after their show at the Frontier was over near the end of 1967. I felt in my gut that my marriage to Don was done, done, done… but I had to know that in my head and my heart too.

The whole year of 1968 is a blur to me now. In addition to some TV jobs I had in Hollywood, doing the Femme de Paris show in Anaheim, and selling my Vegas house, I made several trips to Europe to see Ladi. I had to be sure. Was it really, forever-over with Don? Was my life just starting again with Ladi? My head was pointing me to Don and my Hollywood life, but my heart pointed straight at Ladi…my beautiful, talented Schroeder. I didn't know whether to exit stage right...or left. I loved both Don and Ladi for different reasons and in different ways. I just didn't know what the hell to do.

Back and forth, back and forth to Europe; I had enough peanuts on the planes to last me a lifetime. I'd come home to L.A. and try one more time with Don, but he absolutely wasn't willing to do anything to work on our marriage. I'd go back to Europe, and Ladi treated me like a princess. I think it's interesting that Ladi is the only man I loved, or even cared about at all, that was not a lot older than me. I thought I was always and only attracted to older guys, but Ladi was eight years younger than me. And he was The One! When we first met, he was only 22 years old! But that "kid" knew how to take care of a woman—believe me when I tell you this! Don made me feel ugly, and Ladi made me feel beautiful again.

My visits to Europe were getting longer, and my decision was getting a lot clearer in the summer of 1968. I decided that I needed to earn my own keep over there. I wanted my own money, and I needed to work—I was not used to being unemployed. I didn't really want to spend Don's money to find out if I wanted to dump him—that just didn't seem fair. (Maybe there was some kind of justice in spending his money on my "Medford, not Medford, Medford, not Medford..." dilemma, but still...it just didn't feel right.) Ladi set up a meeting for me with Te-Pravda and Stern, who published magazines and newspapers. At the end of that meeting, I was Lisa Medford, photojournalist, assigned to cover musical concerts and film festivals around Europe. Damn nice gig! With the camera and my journalist credentials opening up doors and borders to this American, I went all around Europe with Ladi—snapping pictures, writing articles, and thoroughly enjoying my personal rebirth…and Ladi!

One day, we returned to his house (his mother's house, actually) from a multi-stop trip to wash clothes, re-pack, refuel, and take off again to attend a Polish Film Festival. We had driven from Prague to Austria to Italy to Yugoslavia and then back to Prague. (Just before we entered Prague, I had noticed that a movie was being shot right outside the city. The movie was *The Bridge at Remagen*, starring George Segal, Ben Gazzara, and Robert Vaughn. Since it was about World War II, there were lots of German and American tanks rolling around on the set. Hmmm…setting up a war zone for themselves, I thought. That might be interesting to watch. No…don't go there, Lisa. That's Medford type of territory.)

Two days after we returned from Yugoslavia, Ladi had to leave for Poland with the other musicians, but I was going to take a commercial plane the following day. Ladi left early in the morning, and I had the day to myself to rest, think, and continue to roam through the beautiful streets of Prague. It was a beautiful day in August—so perfect for walking and exploring.

I had told Ladi's mother that I'd be glad to do the day's shopping, which generally took over an hour since each item came from its own specialty store. I wasn't in a hurry on that gorgeous morning, and I stopped a few times to take pictures of interesting houses and people along my way. I had already filled my bag with bread, cheeses, and lunch meats, but I also made a long (and kind of expensive) stop at the Tuzek's store, which was like an actual department store. You could buy anything at Tuzek's in one spot. They had clothes, BMWs, TVs, corn flakes, and Czech Coca-Cola (that tasted like dog piss). There was a problem in that you could only shop at Tuzek's with Western currency, but luckily I had plenty of that. There's just nothing like buying fun things to raise a girl's spirits!

As I wandered in and out of markets, I had lots to think about. On our last trip together, Ladi had been talking more and more about getting married, but that would mean living in Europe and being away from my family. That would be the least-wonderful part of being married to Ladi. (Of course, there was that "trivial" detail to work out—that I was still married to Medford. Oh well...I knew my way around the Divorce Court in L.A.) As I strolled along, I remember thinking, "I could do this. I could live in this gorgeous city in this beautiful country, as long as I have Ladi. I do love Ladi, and I'm really starting to love this city. I think I could stay here forever."

A few hours later, all I wanted to do was to get the hell out of there!

My "Prague is so perfect" day was suddenly disrupted by the sounds of shouting and gunfire and huge vehicles. What the hell was this? I could see people running in the streets—some of them were carrying guns! There were tanks coming right down the road! Okay, I know what this is...they just moved that movie shoot into town. It's pretty weird not to set up barricades and lights, but they must be filming. No, wait a damn minute—those aren't the German and American tanks I saw the day before. Those are Russian tanks!

The Russians had picked my perfect day of August 21, 1968, to invade Czechoslovakia. Damn inconsiderate! I immediately began to take pictures. I hadn't been a photojournalist for very long, but I sure as hell knew a story when I saw one! While I was snapping pictures of the tanks rolling down the street, I felt a burn on my left arm. Jesus Christ! I've been shot! Thank God, the bullet only grazed me, but I had blood running down my arm!

I continued to take pictures as three armed soldiers came running up to me. They must have been Russian soldiers, but they looked like kids! Kid-like or not, they had rifles, and they were definitely coming after me. I started hollering, "American, American, American!" One of them had his rifle in the air, like he was going to hit me with it, but stopped when he heard "American." They grabbed my camera and ran off...and I ran off in the opposite direction back to Ladi's.

Ladi's mother patched up my wound, and we got Ladi on the phone in Poland. Many phone calls later, he gave me directions to a small airfield on the outskirts of the city. He had arranged for a small plane to get me out of Prague, but we couldn't use the main airport. That was the first place the Russians captured. I was at the airfield early to get the hell out of that war zone! Photojournalism was fun, but I did not intend to be a war correspondent or some casualty in some fucked-up Communist takeover!

That marked the beginning of the end for me and my Schroeder. Ladi and his brother had both been dissenters and had signed a manifest condemning Communism. When the Soviets took over, all the dissenters and their families were in danger. Although I kept in touch with Ladi and went over a few more times to see him after things calmed down, our marriage plans were over. He had to marry a horse-faced Communist shrew who was picked out for him, or his family would be rounded up and imprisoned. Ladi did what he needed to do for his family.

It's been a long time since my plans to be with my Schroeder forever were run over by Soviet tanks. But even now, once in awhile, the scar on my arm will tingle a little…and I remember Ladi.

My love life after Ladi became my "You're fun to be with, and I care something about you, but we're never, ever getting married" life. I got my anticlimactic divorce from Medford. He continued his marrying spree, and I had (mostly) enjoyable relationships with different guys…until they disrespected me, bored me, or tried to get me to marry them. Then…Lisa was out of there!

I had a strange on-and-off relationship with Johnny Rivers and even worked as his manager for awhile. I had actually dated Johnny when I lived in the Beresford Apartments (after Mike Mancuso, before Don Medford, and during Cary Grant.) We drifted apart, but then he came back into my life, after Medford, when I lived on Norton Street. Only this time around, he was rich! Johnny had a gorgeous home and had a full-time cook. Damn good thing, since he was a big-time vegetarian who wouldn't even eat an egg. Fucked up eating habits, but….

One night, we were at my place and had been making love on the floor when Johnny suddenly started laughing. "This is too funny, Lisa. Here we are, back where we started—fucking on the floor like when we were poor!" He was funny, but definitely a little nutty too. He went from drugs to Buddha to Jesus and was a fanatic about all of it!

It took a long time for me to remember the good parts of the Medford Era, and to get over Ladi. Part of me is still trying to balance the good with the bad of Medford, and sometimes I think I'm still trying to get over Ladi. Some things just don't come easy.

But…through all the turmoil and indecision and series of really questionable decisions I made, I knew that I had to keep moving on. I had to be whatever it was that Lisa was changing into…and I needed to hear more applause. I just had to figure out where it was going to come from.

EIGHT

Lisa's '70s Show

Another Decade of Livin' Large

"I don't want to hurt your feelings, Lisa, because you're not that bad an actress. But someday, you're going to find out that your talent lies behind the camera and not in front of it."

Frank Barclay Cleaver shared this insight as he dropped me off after a day of shooting at the studio for a part in a silly spaceship show that he'd written and was producing. It wasn't common practice to hitch rides from the writer/producer, but Frank wasn't just a successful TV writer for *Bonanza* (and others); he was also a dear friend. I had met him during my married-to-Medford days, and we hit it off instantly. At one point in our friendship, I thought I could feel a romantic connection coming on, but what I was feeling must have been indigestion. I should have known that Frank was gay. He was absolutely gorgeous, and he was kind, thoughtful, and generous. Besides those universally admirable traits, he liked to shop with me, and he lived in West Hollywood. Duh, Lisa. Oh well, it was better to have him as a friend. Friends last. Lovers...not so much.

My gay-dar should have been working with Frank. I had certainly known and been friends with lots of gay men: most of the male dancers in Vegas, all my makeup guys, and just about every male model that I'd worked with. When I was married to Don, he directed a number of *Dr. Kildare* episodes, and I became really good friends with Richard Chamberlain. He and I had a ball going shoe shopping, stopping for brunch, shopping some more, having lunch, hitting the stores again… you get the idea. I certainly had no issues with gay men at all. They were great fun and great companions, and I didn't have to worry about them hitting on me. You can't ask for much more than that.

Because it was my friend Frank telling me that I should take a hard look at my acting talent, I wasn't too upset. Okay, I was a little irritated, and I didn't exactly know what he meant, so I just filed his comment away to think about later. I knew that if Frank sold the pilot to the network, I'd have a running part in spite of not being "that bad an actress." Maybe I wasn't great, but Frank and I did have fun shopping Fred Segal's together, and that counted for something!

It was probably time to look at my uncharted road through life though, and re-invent myself. One of my favorite movie lines was Vivien Leigh's in *Gone with the Wind.* As Scarlett, she said, "I can't think about that right now. If I do, I'll go crazy. I'll think about that tomorrow." I'd practice saying those lines in a mirror whenever another life choice would come up. That avoidance technique had served me pretty well through a couple of marriages and Vegas and Hollywood. I'd just give life a little more time, and something wonderful was bound to happen!

But that was then, and this was now—the start of the 1970s. Frankly, I was a little tired of tripping over branches in my life road and stepping in dog shit. I wondered if life would be a little easier if I actually made a plan and followed it. The '70s were a decade of re-branding—changing who Lisa Medford had been into...I'm not sure what. (I'm not even sure what all that '70s stuff was about when I wander down memory lane today.) One thing hadn't changed. I was still following Plan B: just come to a fork in the road and head down the path without knowing what was at the end. What I did know was that more of Lisa's Wild Rides were coming up!

I made some good zigs and some not-so-wonderful zags during the '70s. A high priority for me was to retool the way I looked. I had been a knock-out topless showgirl with the same tits I was born with, but now...it was time to shore those babies up. (If God didn't want us to use silicone, he wouldn't have let us invent it.)

I wanted to pick the right set of boobs though because I had seen some really ugly ones! I didn't need crooked nipples or tits that felt like bowling balls. While I was doctor shopping, my sister Karen suggested that I check out Barbi Benton's new boobs because "they're the best!" Although Barbi was going with Hugh Hefner at the time and primarily living at the Playboy mansion, she also kept her own apartment. (Barbi was then and still is today, nobody's fool. She knew what worked. Make sure you have your own place to rest, revitalize, and maybe to retreat to. You just never know when the "forever" in "it will be wonderful forever" will be over.)

Karen and I went to Barbi's so I could see her new breasts. Barbi didn't care; she was real proud of her newly acquired assets. Karen was right. Not only was Barbi one of the cutest girls in Hollywood, she had the absolute best breasts even though she'd gone from a B cup to a D, which is a really big leap and usually results in grapefruit-looking tits. (Her breasts were so good, they shouldn't even be called "boobs"—they were "breasts.") So I went to Barbi's doctor, and I have to say—I got my money's worth! It's been over 35 years now, and my breasts are still where they're supposed to be. (A limo driver I worked with in Vegas 30 years later was exactly one year younger than my boobs. We celebrated their birthdays together. I still give my boobs a party every year and celebrate with a new, expensive body lotion. Some things you just need to treasure.)

I've referred over a dozen other women to that plastic surgeon, and we all ended up with the same great tits. I've never been concerned that all of us have matching boobs. Who's going to know? What are the chances that we'd all be topless at the same time?

So, I knew I wanted new tits, but that was about all I knew for sure. What should I do with my life? What a boring question. For a good number of months, I used my tested process of, "I'll think about that tomorrow." I had plenty of bailout money from Medford, so I wasn't in a great hurry to start yet another career. What was more important to me, post-Medford, was to find the next wonderful place to live. I knew I needed another Beresford-type environment. Life was always sweeter when "coming home" meant exciting people were around and the party was going on or about to start.

Okay, so Don Medford and Malibu beach houses were out. Where should Lisa live? It was obvious that I was going to have to "tend to business" without a lot of help. It's amazing how many friends you lose when you get divorced from a top Hollywood director. Post-Medford, I lived for a short time on Norton Avenue. The only really good thing was that my friend, Gerri Nelson, came with me. She was dating Max Julien then, a black actor with the best speaking voice in the industry, who was (and actually still is) the epitome of "cool." (In fact, Benilde Little, who wrote the 1999 best-selling novel *The Itch*, described her central character as being "Max Julien cool." Nice.)

Gerri was crazy about Max, but she was worried about letting things get too serious. Dating a black guy was not real acceptable during that decade, even if the guy was a successful actor and an incredible hunk. Gerri didn't worry about what her friends thought; we all thought Max was the best-looking thing we'd seen in a long time! I still remember that smile, the silky skin, those high cheekbones, and the dimples. Damn! That guy was gorgeous! No, it wasn't her friends that had Gerri worried—it was her parents' probable reaction that had her flipping out. I really intended to help her be less worried about this, but I just couldn't resist messing with her a little. (Gerri was the sweetest and craziest girl in the world and the "sixth Malouf sister" for her entire life, but she was more than a little gullible.)

"Gerri, why are you so worried? Max isn't even black-black. He could be an Indian or maybe Persian. Besides, he's so gorgeous. Wouldn't your parents want beautiful grand-kids?" I asked her.

That wasn't helpful. "Lisa, you know that my parents would freak out over anything but a lily-white guy," Gerri replied. "What if we got married and our baby was really black? My parents would kill me!"

I consoled Gerri with this tidbit from my vast repository of superior knowledge. "Gerri, don't you know that all babies are born white? They don't turn black for three days. They oxidize in the air. Just let your parents see the baby right away and then never again. Problem solved."

Gerri told Max that her parents wouldn't really be a problem because she'd just found out that babies don't turn black until they oxidize after they're born. His response was, "Did Medford tell you that shit?"

Actually, that was his response to all the shit I told Gerri. Like the time we were coming home from the County Fair in Pomona. We'd gone to see the horse races, but the Fair race track was so hokey! It looked like a bunch of little plastic horses running around my kitchen table. It was raining on and off, and we decided to just blow off the last of the races.

In the parking lot of the Fair, it started to rain again, and by the time we got on the freeway, it was pouring. Gerri asked, "Why does it seem to rain harder on the freeway?" I couldn't pass that up.

"It just seems like it's raining harder because we're going faster. If you're going 30 mph, then the rain hits at 1,236 drops per square foot. But if you drive at 60 mph, you're passing through two times more square feet, so it seems to be raining harder, but it could actually be raining less on the freeway."

"Oh," she replied. "That makes sense." Poor, sweet Gerri!

She got the usual response from Max when she shared that piece of newly-acquired knowledge with him. "Did Medford tell you that shit?"

Another friend who joined Gerri and me on Norton Ave. was Joanna Frank. Joanna Frank was really Joanna Bochco. She was an actress and the sister of Steven Bochco, who ended up getting a basketful of Emmy nominations and awards for

Hill Street Blues, L.A. Law, and *NYPD Blue*. When Joanna lived with us on Norton, Steven was still building his credentials as a writer and producer (and was often short on cash), so to us, he was just the nice, quiet guy who used to crash on our couch regularly. Who knew that Steven Bochco would be the creative genius behind all those popular shows?

Joanna had played the starring role of the queen bee in the *Outer Limits* episode titled "ZZZZZ." The part had been specifically written for her by Joseph Stefano, and she really played a great bee that turned into a human. Unfortunately, there weren't a lot more flying insect parts out there, and although she was a fine actress (and gorgeous), Joanna didn't get a lot of parts during the '70s. (She did really well in the '80s and '90s though, when she teamed up, in more than one way, with Alan Rachin and her brother Steven. Joanna married Alan in 1978 and subsequently played Sheila Brackman, the wife of Alan's character, Douglas, in many episodes of *L.A. Law*—which was created by her brother Steven. Joanna and Alan are still married today. Nice when things work out like that. Obviously her husband appreciated her talents and supported her acting career. Unlike a director I knew, named Don Medford.)

Joanna Frank was my roommate when she wasn't sleeping with Michael Callan. Michael's days of being a "heartthrob actor" were just about over by then, but he was still making good rounds off screen with the women.

A few years later, when my sister Karen planned to marry Callan, I said, "Don't do that! Don't marry an actor! Never marry an actor. All they care about is the spotlight and the applause. They're too needy. You'll have a whole life of massaging his back and his ego at the same time! Anyway, he was sleeping with Joanna Frank while he was still married to his first wife."

"But I think he has great potential," Karen told me. Sure, great potential to be a loser. But what did I know? So she married—and divorced him.

After a brief stint on Norton Ave., I moved into a great El Centro apartment on the corner of Santa Monica Boulevard and Vine, in what had become a seedy part of L.A. It only cost $125 a month, which got me one of the apartments in the four duplexes in the little complex. At one time, that whole area had been very upscale and elegant, with fabulous apartments and hotels surrounded by large areas of orange groves and park-like empty spaces. Seriously famous people had frequented the El Centro area—like Mae West, who lived for a long time in a neighborhood hotel. And some seriously interesting animals lived there too.

Errol Flynn had starred in *Kim* in India in 1950 and was really fascinated with elephants. (I think it was their big trunks.) Anyway, some executive from the movie wanted to give him a memento and decided that the perfect gift was an elephant. Now, what the hell was he thinking? "I wonder if Errol would like a nice pen set, or maybe a set of cufflinks with *Kim* engraved on them? No—I know! I'll give him an elephant! Something that weighs three tons, eats all day long, and shits everywhere! Yeah—that's the perfect gift!" It doesn't matter what industry we're talking about—there are crazy people everywhere!

So Errol got the elephant, and he kept it on the grounds around the El Centro apartments for awhile and finally gave it to John Carradine. (I heard that Carradine finally got tired of paying someone to follow the elephant around with a crap bucket and gave it to a zoo.)

The area may have gone bad with a musical instrumental rental place, a Carpeteria, and too many Mexican bars and restaurants cropping up around my building, but time hadn't damaged the duplexes. The old Hollywood glamour was still alive and well in those apartments. They were spectacular—the kind of place that I was supposed to have. Each apartment had gleaming hardwood floors and all-stucco walls, with hand-painted Spanish tiles around the fireplaces. The living room was to die for with walls that were two stories tall. The ceiling (actually the roof) over the living room was wire-grid glass, and the outside wall was floor-to-ceiling skinny windows. It looked and felt like you were living outside! (Those windows and the skylights were what attracted lots of artists. David Carradine had his art studio there for many years.) The full daylight was like living in the spotlight all the time (which was pretty nice), but it wasn't so great for closing the drapes at night. Oh well—you can't have everything.

One of the more interesting and lovely neighbors on El Centro was Ilona von Montagh, who was Bela Lugosi's second wife (of five total). She spoke with an old-country accent, looked like a 100-year-old grandma doll, and took me under her wing while I was there. She was really frail, so I would take her shopping or pick up things at the market for her, and then she'd cook for me. I ate a lot of Hungarian boiled cabbage dishes on El Centro. They reminded me of my grandmother's Lebanese cabbage rolls, only Ilona's were better because she added sour cream. (I was careful not to tell my grandmother that.)

Ilona would tell me stories about Lugosi and his start in Hollywood, but with her thick accent, I didn't get a lot of what she said. I did get the story about how Lugosi's marriage to Beatrice Weeks only lasted three days, though. Ilona delighted in telling me how Lugosi had married Weeks for her considerable money, but then she found out he was having an affair with Clara Bow and dumped him in three days. That was a killer scandal in 1929. (That's sure different from today, when getting married and then annulled during a boring, three-day weekend in Vegas is just something to pass the time.) Ilona would just cackle her tiny little butt off every time she told me about that—which was often. She'd say, "He had no time for getting the money. Just get in her panties and then go—out the door!" That just cracked her up!

Of course, another regular on El Centro was Deirdre Flynn, who would be in and out, like she was at the Beresford and everywhere else I ever lived—up to and including today, almost 40 years later. Deirdre really was a lot of fun back then (as she still is today), so she was always welcomed into the party. In fact, she was usually the instigator of the parties, if not the chief consumer of all party treats—the legal ones and the not-so-legal.

One day, I was home alone (which was pretty unusual in itself) when someone started banging on my door. We had those little security windows in our doors at El Centro, but when I looked out, I couldn't see anything. Something was blocking it. Okay, I'm game. I'll open the door. (It didn't occur to me instantly that the old Jewish guy in our building had been killed by someone who snuck in when he left a brick in the door while he and his wife went to temple.)

When I opened the door, I found a huge dildo stuck in the window frame—sticking straight out like a stallion in heat! Biggest damn dildo I ever saw. Now, in other circumstances, I would have figured I needed to thank someone for such a considerate gift. But stuck in my door? I didn't even know how to get it out. I sure didn't want to touch it. Who knew where that thing had been before it was dangling off my door? I grabbed a stray sock that was in the living room, pulled the dildo out of the window frame, and walked right around to the garbage bin and dumped it, along with the sock. For just a few seconds, I thought, "Hmmm...do you want to throw this away, Lisa? It's really a great looking dildo." Thankfully, hygienic concerns prevailed, and out it went. I was totally freaked out. Someone stuck that thing on my door, and now I had a sock in the living room without a mate. Shit.

It took me years to find out who had done that. The tipoff was when Deirdre gave me a ginormous pink dildo wrapped in a huge pink bow for a birthday gift. As soon as I saw it, I knew...she was the dildo leaver. Then she told me how she and her friends had hid behind a bush to watch my reaction. They thought it was priceless. Sure...priceless.

While I was at El Centro, another "love of my life," Scot Varley, moved in with me—the day that I met him. We were together for about six years, but I never had any intention of marrying him. My sister Barbara asked me, "What do you see in that Scot? What is he anyway? He looks like an ad for men's underwear." Okay, Barbara...and you need to ask what I see in him?

Scot was fun, and the sex was great, but like I told you, after Medford, I decided not to be a "wife" again. Although

I did like having someone around to cook for and fuss over, I never liked the quickie ceremonies in Vegas, I never got enough presents, and I just didn't see the need for having a husband. As the old saying goes—why buy the pig when the sausage is free?

Besides being Lisa-worthy, the El Centro apartment was about five blocks from my work. (*News about my new job is coming up. Hang in here.*) In spite of (and in addition to) all my partying and after-hours socializing, doing my job was always first on my list.

I really enjoyed El Centro, but after awhile things started changing in my life. (And that would be different from... when?) I was starting my own company, which meant moving to a different work location. Sister Joey and her husband, Loren Judd, had just purchased a new home, and they left a killer apartment that I really wanted to have. In addition to those really good reasons for finding and packing up boxes (again!), I was getting real tired of cabbage.

My next move was to 125 North Sweetzer Avenue, into a gorgeous art-deco building. It had eight, one-bedroom units at the time, and all my friends would move in and out, either into my apartment or into one of the others. They'd just keep switching around, sampling all of the apartments—and the next was even better than the last. Gerri moved in when an apartment opened up across the hall from mine, and other friends would come in as soon as more apartments were available. Gerri and I were gathering all our friends together again.

Somewhere in this to-ing and fro-ing with the apartments, I decided it was a good idea to use cocaine. I'm making it

sound like I actually thought it out. That would be...not.
It's not like I weighed the pros and cons and made a fully-
informed decision; it was there, and it felt right at the time.

Somehow I had missed the whole drug scene in the '60s.
I didn't mean to miss out. But while my friends were knee
deep in Zig Zag papers, I was just busy zigging and zag-
ging. Besides, I sure didn't need any "enhancer" in the '60s
to have a good time. Between livin' large in Vegas and being
a Hollywood darling (and rich), I had all the enhancement I
could handle. But the '70s needed a little more "glitter." It
certainly was readily available, and it did look like clean white
snow, so how bad could it be for me?

One thing I didn't like about coke was the price! That was
bullshit—paying for stuff to stick up my nose when I could be
buying Louis Vuitton bags, Gucci shoes, and Limoges china?
I knew what to do when I wanted my own stash of...whatever.
Sell the shit, and get my own inventory free. I certainly had
a huge potential customer list: everybody who was showing
up at my apartments regularly for the ongoing party! Cocaine
was a "staple." Set out trays of those little hot dogs in BBQ
sauce and some cheese and fancy crackers, make some tabouli,
uncork the wine, and get out the coke. Instant party.

The business model of "sell to others and get my own shit
free" worked really well for me in the '60s when I (and everyone else I knew) was hooked on wearing wigs. The good ones
weren't cheap! But that didn't stop me from wanting a few
dozen for myself. Easy solution—I'll set up a wig company.
(*I think I forgot to tell you about my wig company in the '60s. Sorry
about that...just stay with me. I'll be coming back to '70s cocaine
days in a minute.*)

At the same time as all my other career paths in the '60s—showgirl, actress, model, wife—I also set up and ran Nona Lisa's Wigs with my friend Susan Banas. There was money in selling wigs, for sure, and my company made a healthy profit for several years along with providing me with several heads of hair. When the fascination with wigs died down, we just stopped the wig company and moved on.

I actually moved on to opening a little antique store called Mrs. Robinson's Behind. (I still love that name. *The Graduate* had opened just in time for me to use the name, and my shop was "behind" another one. Susan Banas, Judy Richmond, and Deborah Walley (who played Gidget in *Gidget Goes Hawaiian* and was voted Photoplay's Most Popular Actress in 1961) owned the shop in front.) The primary reason I opened Mrs. Robinson's Behind was to get rid of some of the stuff I had bought with all the acting, modeling, showgirl, wig, and Medford money. It was nice stuff, but just how many sets of dishes does one person need? Not 19 sets—somebody needed to buy about nine of those! As soon as I dumped my excess treasures, I just closed out that venture too. None of us girls ever made a bunch of money with our shops, but we sure had a good time! Young guys would regularly show up at my shop asking to meet "Mrs. Robinson," and sometimes…they did.

Cocaine actually served me really well in the '70s. When I did coke, I had big tits and big hair, and I was thin. I quit the coke in the '80s, and everything else went to hell—boobs were still big, but the hair went bad, and I gained weight. Damn. But I had to quit because the shit was no good any more. It was coming in on some dumbass donkey's back and they were sticking stuff in it. You started pulling sugar boogies out of your nose. (I know; that's a really bad image!) Before the suppliers got greedy and started doctoring it, I used to keep my coke bottle in a Louis Vuitton bag by my bed. I'd watch the 11 o'clock news, snort a little, and go out like a light. Life was good. But not after the '70s. Men, food, drugs—if you don't feel good about it—don't do it!

Besides the product going bad in the late '70s, I got real tired of everybody else's paranoia. It seemed like overnight, I was expected to meet my customers in the middle of the damn night, in some crappy neighborhood, in the pouring rain! What was that? We had to sneak around like everybody didn't already know that everybody in Hollywood did coke?

Another thing that made me crazy about my drug-dealing enterprise was that somehow I had become the resident expert on "Selling Drugs for Fun and Profit." Too many rookie deal-ers were coming to the mountaintop to seek my counsel on all aspects of selling drugs. "Should I let a customer test the shit first? What about refunds—do I have to do that? Will it go bad if I keep it in the refrigerator—should I try to keep it away from the onions? Do you think I can charge more if I decorate the bags?" These girls thought they should be selling drugs? No, no, no. They were not the brightest bulbs on the marquee.

The last straw came when I got a call from an acquain-tance (not a friend—she was way too stupid to be a friend of mine) who wanted "advice on how to break into the business." I said, "Hey, dealing drugs is not a corporate position. You don't need to prepare a resume. Just buy some shit and sell it."

"Oh, okay. But can you help me figure this out. Is a quar-ter bag bigger or smaller than an eighth?"

My answer was, "Well, that depends. Are you selling or buying?"

"Hmmm…that's a good question." While she was thinking that out, I told myself, "That's it, Lisa! These people are just too fucked up! Make them go away!" I knew she'd be pondering my pearl of wisdom for a very long time, so I just walked away from the phone. Thirty minutes later, I went back and hung up. I don't know—she could have still been on the phone trying to work out those options.

Once I got a call from some guy asking me if I just had an old baggie that he could scrape. That did it! Bad product, shitty customers, too much wet hair, and too many sleepless nights—I needed to get out of that business. So, I did.

There was at least one educational opportunity from my days (years) of selling drugs. I learned the metric system. I didn't want to have anything to do with metrics before I needed to learn it for my "trade." Meters and kilograms and Celsius temperatures—that shit was just too hard. Besides, it got started in France. Hello! Look around. Are we French? French people needed to stick with designing clothes and making cheese. But suddenly, knowing how much a gram was became an important business requirement. Too much product in an eight ball of cocaine, and there goes your profit! It just goes to show—there are learning opportunities to enhance your personal growth and betterment in all activities. *Do you know the metric system yet? An eight ball is one eighth of an ounce, which equals about 3.5 grams. There ya go…now I've helped you with your math. If someone asks you what you got out of this book, you can add "a metric conversion lesson" to the list*

Somewhere in those years, I decided that I needed something steady to do. I had always worked hard (and as you can tell, at many different things at once), but now I had too much downtime. I was still buying $600 boots and $1,000 dresses—and that was in 1970s money. *You think I spent too much on clothes? You should have seen my furs "budget!"* I wasn't yet to the point where I needed to think about missing a spree at Fred Segal's, but I did want to do some real work. My acting gigs were too hit-and-miss. That was irritating. I never figured that I'd be a star, and I certainly didn't want to become a full-fledged celebrity, but in my late 30s I was no longer in demand for bit parts? Even with my great new tits? That was the shits!

Maybe I should pull out that advice from Frank Cleaver. Maybe my real talent was behind the camera instead of in front of it.

How Cool: Lisa Medford, Producer

Through a series of "I know someone who knows someone" encounters, I started work for $400 a month as an "assistant" for Maher, Kaump, and Clark, a well-known Hollywood advertising agency. I was working in the Train-Aid Department, which made (primarily) medical educational film strips. (*Do you even know what a film strip is? It's like a bunch of still photos joined together to make the story. Nothing moves around by itself. The speed of the story often depends on how fast you set up the "advance" button on the projector. If you didn't know about film strips, that's okay. I just did the math again. That was almost 40 years ago! Hmmm. That makes me tired just thinking about it. I'm going to lie down for awhile. I'll catch up with you later.*)

Anyway, as an assistant, my job was to do…whatever was needed to get the assignment done and make life easier for the producers. It didn't take more than a few days to see that securing the right talent at the right price was a royal pain in the butt. There were too many phone calls and too few actors who wanted to take the time for a one-day shoot or a voiceover that wouldn't add much luster to their resumes. Since they didn't really know these actors, Train-Aid would sometimes need to audition 20 people just to find the right actor to play a fat, diabetic guy or the perfect voice to play an English doctor. Getting the right talent meant knowing who was out there, who was available, and what they could do, and it required getting them to show up for a quick, not-great-pay shoot—sober. The whole casting task used to be a time-consuming and expensive process for Train-Aid—until Lisa Malouf Medford showed up!

I explained to my new bosses that they should put me in charge of securing talent. In just a few more days, I had figured out what had to be done to finish the backlog of film strips that Train-Aid had when I arrived. This is what I had to know to pull off my "I can source the talent faster and better than anyone else" claim.

One: Find a whole bunch of actors who could show up quickly (and on time) for a not-too-exciting gig. My knowing everyone in Hollywood, and letting half of the "between-job" actors in town camp out on my couch, had already served me well for getting my own modeling and acting jobs. Now, my tumor-sized Rolodex file was about to pay off in my new career.

"I can save you a ton of time and money by calling in all my actor friends. We just need to pay them $50 cash, under the table, for the shoot. Most of them are on unemployment most of the time, and for $50? They'll be lining up." And they were lining up. For three weeks solid, our hallways were full while I made the lists of who could play or voice which parts in the filmstrips and when.

Don't be thinking that I filled up Train-Aid with never-to-be-heard-about-again losers. Have you heard about any of these guys: Les Tremayne (*General Hospital*), Hans Conried (Uncle Tonoose on *Make Room for Daddy*), Marvin Miller (*The Millionaire*), or Michael Callan (*Cat Ballou*)? They were just a few of my preferred actors. Even the stars who seemed to be filming movies and TV series regularly were out of work a lot. (Those Tours of Movie Star Houses were a joke in Hollywood. If anyone wanted to see a bunch of celebrities, all they had to do was hang out at the Unemployment Office. All the stars would show up there at some time or another.)

Two: Know what to listen to and look for to pick great voiceover people. The pictures were shot separately, and then the voices and narration were added. The actors in the photos and the voices weren't necessarily the same person, but they needed to sound like they went together.

I had learned to spot the best people from watching TV. I knew that no matter how small the part, I had to have a pro. I had heard Don say often, "Even the smallest part done badly will make the whole show not believable." Now, I was the one who needed to pay attention to diction, accents, rhythm, and pace. Listening hard to discover who made loud breathing sounds was a critical factor. I didn't need someone who sounded like they were nearing orgasm right in the middle of a film on pancreatic cancer.

I also knew that I needed to make it as easy as possible for my actors to give me their best. This was another Medford lesson. Don was called the "actor's director" because he understood what it took to get the best of them and tried to give them all the support they needed.

Doing medical film strips was a new experience for many of my actors. Although they were all professionals, they all weren't used to so many medical terms, which meant some advance preparation on my part. I realized this the first time I heard a top actor say "bid" when he saw "b.i.d." After that, I wrote "twice a day" next to that acronym on every script for every filmstrip.

Three: Know who was likely to be sober and not high on any given day. It was a real advantage that I was also selling drugs during this time. A large number of the people on my talent list were also my after-hours clients.

If I'd made a big delivery to an actor at midnight the night before, chances were he'd show up the next day sniffing. You could sure wreck the ambiance of a story on bowel obstruction when the doctor was sniffing all through his lines.

Sometimes, I'd use this information in reverse too though. The coke heads were sometimes really good for a grieving patient or parent. All that sniffing made them sound really sad. That's one of the extras I brought to the job. I knew how to match up the talent, along with their sometimes-not-so-great kinks, to the demand.

Four: Understand what it takes to make a storyline out of teenage acne or adrenal gland tumors or kidney infections. For this one, I reached into my "Things I got from Medford" trick bag (which was pretty slim, actually) and remembered watching him block out scripts. I quickly learned to think about the order the images (scenes) needed to be in to keep the story going in the right direction. I had to position the actors to fill up the frames to keep the focus where it should be.

Medford had taught me (unknowingly) how to block a story, and the head scriptwriter at Train-Aid, Charles Wright-Cromer, taught me to match the images to the words. He said, "Writing a script is just like hanging out clothes to dry. If you have great pictures, they're the clothes line. Now pin the words to the line. If you have a great story, then the words are the clothesline. Just pin those pictures to the words." Easy. Yeah, easy when he did it!

A few years earlier, when Don's mother was dying in Florida, he needed to be there with her. It was right in the middle of filming a *Fugitive* episode, and "the show must go on." Don handed me the script, and said, "You need to work with Judd Taylor (his replacement) on this and get David Janssen to do what I need him to do." Not a problem, until David Janssen was not doing what Don would have wanted him to do. Janssen invited me to his trailer for "lunch." Evidently, *lunch* meant *fucking* to Janssen. What a toad! He was married, and I was married to the director, for Christ's sake! Not on your life.

But, in that *Fugitive* experience, I was able to get right inside what a director did. The "doing" was even better than just watching. Combining what I'd learned from my multiple "lives" with my universe-sized circle of people let me deliver what I'd promised to Train-Aid—faster, cheaper, better film strips. In 37 days I went from a $400-a-month assistant to a

$2,400-a-month producer/director/editor, with my own office and a secretary. Life was good again.

As the producer, I was in charge of spending (or not spending) the money, as well as being the director, editor, and talent person. It all came together; I had the responsibility for making and sticking to the budgets, which included securing the right people for the right story for the right price and getting to a salable product.

One of our jobs was a 30-second PSA spot for blind people. I arranged to have Tom Sullivan do the voice. I had never met him—imagine that, someone who hadn't slept on my couch—but I knew that he was a blind pianist, composer, singer, actor, and writer. He was a Renaissance man with a great voice.

Charles was a little irritated. "How's he going to read the announcement? I don't write scripts in Braille!"

"Not to worry," I said. I'll read it to him a few times. Everyone says he's real smart. How hard can it be for him to remember 30 seconds' worth of words?"

I went to Tom's office, and after a little yacky-yacky talk, he said, "I'd like to touch your face to see what you look like." Sure, touch away. Tom ran his fingers over my face. Then he took my hands and felt my long porcelain nails.

"Wow, you're a real girly girl, aren't you?"

Tom went right from the nails to my boobs and grabbed one in each hand. I squealed a little in surprise, but he just laughed and said, "Sometimes it's great to be blind. I get away with a lot!" Add great sense of humor to all of Tom's other accomplishments.

Another assignment through Maher, Kaump, and Clark was being the assistant producer for two Academy of Country Music Award shows. Those country and western singers were great fun, and they all sounded alike with those too-adorable country accents! After my first ACM show, I went back to Hollywood talkin' country. I've always been a chameleon. I start to sound like whomever I'm hearing talk. That country twang was just too good to pass up!

A stand-out memory is about Loretta Lynn, who was just one of the cutest little country gals I met at those shows. One night backstage, we were talking, and Loretta started wondering, "Why do we get old looking and wrinkled? I don't understand why that only happens to us. Cows don't wrinkle. You can't tell which cows are old or young. Why can't we just age like cows?"

I offered, "I don't know. Maybe we should keep ourselves covered in fur?"

She reached out and patted my fox jacket and said, "Well, you're on the way there, girl!"

A part of the ACM job where I really got to shine was lining up the guest presenters. Again, I went to my cowboy-hat-sized Rolodex and started dialing. (In those days, everybody took Lisa Medford's call!) There was another assistant on the second show with me who I'll call Dana. Dana and I were not tight. She was jealous of me because I could get all the best presenters because I knew them all from my Medford years.

The night before the actual taping with the audience for the second ACM show, she got her revenge for my success.

Dana gave me a bunch of pills and said, "Here, take these in the morning, and they'll make your tummy really flat." I thought that was a pretty nice gesture for her to make since I was always complaining if my tummy stuck out one-sixteenth of an inch.

"Great, thanks! How many do I need—two?"

"No," she advised. "Take all six of them. They'll work better with more."

Can you just feel what's coming up next? Yep, they were laxatives. I missed the first part of the dress rehearsals and barely made it to the show on time. When I showed up, I was practically green, and my butt was killing me from all that cheap hotel toilet paper, but my tummy was flat. Dana just never knew how close she came to being killed. It took me about 20 years to start laughing about the "help" she gave me, but finally, I decided that it really was funny. It was funny that she thought of it, and even funnier that I'd just swallow down whatever someone handed me.

Laughing a lot while I was making films on pancreatic cancer and urinary tract infections was real important to me—for obvious reasons. Unless you are really a weirdo, those aren't topics that a person should be thinking about all day long. I really needed to laugh a lot, and thankfully, there was funny stuff everywhere.

My wonderful, believe-anything friend Gerri gave me a great laugh during that time that I still chuckle about today.

Not long after I'd joined Maher, Kaump, and Clark, Bruce Kaump showed me pictures of the first moon landing. I was showing Gerri the 35mm slides that night, and she said, "Wow! How did they get those shots?"

"Oh, that wasn't a problem," I said. "*Life* magazine sent a photographer up there a few days earlier to set up the shots."

Of course, Gerri told Max Julien how smart it was to get the camera guys there ahead of time to get the shots lined up to record such an historic event. Max said what he always did. "Did Medford tell you that shit?"

"Wax" Clark, Dana (the laxative bitch), real Roy Clark, and Lisa

After a few years though, Train-Aid time was coming to an end. Train-Aid was financed by American Hospital Supply, which, at the time, was the biggest medical supply company in America. But they wanted to get out of the training-film business. I was sad that we were closing because I had made lots of new friends, had eaten well, and had enjoyed a bunch of good laughs. More importantly (as it turned out), I had learned what I needed to know for my next life. Of course, I didn't know the part about preparing for a new life at the time. I was still just traveling down the road, picking my turns by whatever felt good at the time when I got there. I knew something else was going to pop up for me because it always did. And pretty soon, there it was—my new career path. Alice and Icer Malouf's little girl was growing up!

Is that applause I hear in the distance?

NINE

"And the Award Goes to..."

"Lisa, I don't know if you have the time to take on another project, but I'd appreciate it if you'd consider taking this one on. It's important to me personally, but I just can't fit it in. What do you think? Do you have time to produce a documentary?" Time? Yes, that's one thing I did have. Train-Aid had just "wrapped," and I was waiting (and looking a little) for my next Wild Ride.

The person on the phone was Melvin Frank who was a brilliant and highly successful screen writer and producer/director. His work included: *Not With My Wife You Don't, A Funny Thing Happened to Me on the Way to the Forum,* the Bob Hope/ Bing Crosby *Road Shows,* and *Li'l Abner.* Melvin was also a former neighbor. He and his wife had lived across the hall from Don and me in Los Angeles—when there was a Don and me. Melvin Frank wanted me to look at a project? I guess so! That sounded like a potential Wild Ride coming up!

This is what preceded that phone call to me. Once again, Don Medford had called because he needed a ride to some doctor's office. Don's bimbo wife number six wouldn't take him, and he was too sick to drive. (I spent almost the next 30 years getting calls from Don asking for something that his wife du jour wouldn't do. Some things just stick with you like bad

Mexican food.) Anyway, Don must have figured he owed me something, and when Melvin Frank told him that he needed a producer for a small project, Don gave Melvin my number.

Melvin's personal life had more problems than his professional life. I knew from living in the same building with them that his wife was a binge drinker. She wouldn't touch a drop for a year, and then she'd buy three bottles of vodka and down them so fast, she'd just about blow up. But Melvin was really devoted to her and had worked with many rehab facilities and doctors looking for a cure for her. It appeared that he had found the right man who helped her overcome her addition: Dr. Max Schneider. Dr. Schneider wanted to do a documentary, and Melvin wanted to help him out with it, but Frank was just too big a guy (and way too busy) to take on something that small. So, the call to Lisa Medford, the producer/director...of film strips, not films.

There was a considerable difference between doing Train-Aid film strips and doing what Melvin was asking about. But did I want to do it, and did I think I could? Damn straight I did! I didn't mention to Melvin that my experience was film strips, and I also didn't tell him that I didn't have a company, a crew, or even a camera. Details, details... (I had always figured that I could do...whatever. Do you want to split an atom? Sure, I can probably do that. Just find me an atom and a machete.)

The first order of business was to assemble my crew. I knew the secret to pulling this off: find the best people I could, pay them as well as I could, and let them be brilliant! My first call was to my Train-Aid writer, Charles Wright-Cromer. I explained the gig and offered to go 50-50 with him on the new company. He was in!

My second call was to Joe Longo, the cameraman I had worked with on the Academy of Country Music Awards shows. He was an incredibly talented and extremely versatile cameraman. Joe was once in a helicopter photographing some war when the helicopter crashed! He shot the crash all the way to the ground…and obviously walked away, with his film. Joe was in! The next call was to Patrick Thomas Roark. He was not only a great editor; he was also fast, which translated to less cost. That was the third member of my dream team.

Patrick also had an offbeat sense of humor that either left you laughing…or made you want to back slowly out of the room. In his editing suite, there were dozens of empty yellow plastic film spools that he hung from the ceiling on wire. On one of the spools, Patrick had written "My Favorite Spool." When I asked him what that meant, he barely looked up from the editing bay. He just deadpanned, "That's my favorite one." Okay…back out slowly. That's a little weird.

Now that I had the crew, I rented the lights and the sound equipment, Joe brought the camera, and that was the start of my company, Visual Exchange, Inc. I picked that really generic name because I had no clear idea about what this company was going to do after that first film with Dr. Schneider, and I wanted to leave all my doors open. (Thinking about this now, that must have been a sign that I was turning into an adult. That's about the first time that I thought ahead about something. I guess that 37 years old was a good enough age to starting being a grown-up.)

Melvin Frank put me in touch with Dr. Schneider, and we were ready to roll less than two weeks after I heard about the project. That first film was *Medical Aspects of Alcohol* in two parts. Charles had told me that the real money was in distribution, so not only did Visual Exchange do the production, we also set up a separate arm of the company to distribute. (And he was right…that's where the money was!) It must have been a good film because we sold a ka-jillion of them to schools, hospitals, the Department of Defense, and the DMV. For about 12 years after I produced the film in the midseventies, if you got a DUI, you probably watched my film. It was part of the "punishment." (I thought it was pretty funny that I'd let an error in the film slip through to the final, to-be-sold version. Cocaine was misspelled in the film. Now, you'd think that I would have known better!)

Part of our distribution marketing plan involved setting up booths or rooms at conferences for doctors, hospitals, and addiction-control agencies. (The way some of those attendees drank, I wasn't really sure if the conferences were for or against alcoholism.) We included a "come-on," of course, to encourage attendees to view the film. I'd set out a big bowl with a sign that read, "Drop Your Card Here to Win a Trip to Hawaii." It's amazing that the winner of the drawings was always the same person. I had a great time in Hawaii.

That first film with and about Dr. Schneider kicked off Visual Exchange both financially and in reputation. Overnight, I was getting calls from TV stations, and they were taking my calls when I had propositions for them. (No more of the "Mr. Stevens will get back to you when he's not tied up.") And I don't want to brag that I was way ahead of my time when I proposed a "reality" talk show with non-famous people to ABC. Well, yes, I do want to brag about it, but ABC was not as visionary as I was, obviously, and turned that one down. They also rejected my proposal for a documentary on the emerging problem of illegal aliens. Hello! This was 1976!

However, one futuristic proposal that was accepted and that I produced was *Fragments: American Terrorists*. Okay... now this was in the mid-seventies and I was raising the flag about the dangers that were coming! Another project that was both fun and profitable was *In Search of the Bronze Man,* which was about acupuncture. The "bronze man" was a very old statue that had some kind of healing powers and was located in Korea, Taiwan, or Hong Kong. We needed to find it. I was definitely up for that gig; traveling to exotic places on someone else's dime...just like the "old days" of going on location with Medford.

The doctor who wanted this film was Brent Lovejoy from Denver, and he was willing to pay us $30,000 to produce it. Nice money in the '70s! Dr. Lovejoy, Joe, and I headed east to find the bronze guy. We had six Taiwanese guys with us on the first leg of the trip to Seoul, which proved to be really useful when we got there. The flight from L.A. to Seoul should have been really miserable, but we slept most of the way thanks to Dr. Lovejoy and his bottle full of Quaaludes. "Better living through chemistry." We stayed in Seoul for five days—but no bronze man there. So back onto a plane headed for Taiwan.

When we landed, the plane was immediately boarded by military police who started handing out black mourning bands to all of us. Joe, Dr. Lovejoy, and I didn't know why, but when people with guns give you something and everyone else is putting it on, it seemed smart to go along. Finally, the police left the plane, and the Taiwanese guys explained that Chiang Kai-shek had died and that we were all supposed to go to where he was lying in state to pay our respects. Okay, that's a little weird, and I was fairly certain that he wasn't the bronze man we were searching for, but the military police did have guns.

The police took us from the airport right to where Chiang Kai-shek was lying in state—no time to eat or make a bathroom stop and no time to change. I really wanted to change because I was pretty sure that a mauve colored t-shirt with no bra and jeans were not considered formal funeral wear. But the military police didn't seem to care, so I quit worrying about my inappropriate clothes. We saw a way-too-long line with armed soldiers herding the smashed-together people forward when we got there, but for a reason I never found out, we were taken right in and put into seats. We thought they would have made Joe leave his camera at the hotel, but they must have missed seeing it. (Maybe they were distracted by the bra-less t-shirt.) As soon as we got there, Joe started filming—Chiang Kai-shek lying there, the people in line, the soldiers—all of it. I nudged him and mouthed, "Be careful," but that was unnecessary. Joe filmed his own helicopter crash…a few dozen armed soldiers weren't going to scare him off a potential story!

There were what seemed like hundreds of cameramen there, but after taking 80 rolls of film of a dead guy just lying there, there wasn't much else to photograph, so they were mostly just hanging around. After what seemed like a very long time of just sitting there, our "handlers" motioned for us to leave. I watched the other people and knew that we were supposed to stop before passing Chiang Kai-shek and bow. Okay…I can do this. Just walk up and bow for a minute and then get the hell out of there! The sight of an American in a bra-less t-shirt must have triggered something though. As soon as I stopped to bow, the flashes from those hundreds of cameras started going off! Our handlers quickly stepped in, and we all made a fast exit. Worked for me!

After some delay while the whole city went into funeral mode, we finally got out of there and went to Hong Kong, where we found the bronze man. I had been told that there used to be rubies where all the acupuncture points were, but scavengers must have looted those years ago. Now there were red lights in those spots. It looked like modern technology married to ancient medicine. We'd gone all that way to get a few minutes of footage of a huge, old, bronze statue with red lights stuck all over it. Oh well...

When we returned to L.A., Joe said, "Hey, that funeral footage is pretty good. What do you want to do with the film?" I figured we should do what we do with film...sell it to someone. We wanted to get it out there quick while the Taiwanese population in L.A. was still interested in Chiang Kai-shek's death, so we put up posters in China Town, advertised in the Taiwanese newspapers, and sold over 9,000 copies of the film for $25 each! Thanks to Joe's swift camera action, we made a ton of money (accidentally) on that bronze guy project!

Just before searching for the old acupuncture guy, I produced my most important piece. It was another visionary film that I did for ABC-TV: *All Things Being Equal.* The Equal Rights Amendment had been passed by Congress in 1972, and I figured it was time (overdue) for a documentary on women's rights. My twist was that my film gave the "pros" and the "cons" of women's liberation, and showed the conflict between the desire for "liberation" and the newly-discovered problems that were being created by the changes in relationships and in self-image. Dr. James Dobson, (the founder of Focus on the Family) certainly took the "better to stay at home and tend to the family" side of the discussion. Dr. Terry Paulson (today's in-demand speaker on "assertiveness") offered a "blended" approach. I featured interviews with several prominent female executives and women in "men's" jobs such as police work, as well as a few (not too well-paid) "actors," like my manicurist.

All Things Being Equal was what validated that I had arrived as a producer and director. I received an Emmy nomination from the Hollywood Chapter of the National Academy of Television Arts and Sciences as the "Producer of *All Things Being Equal*: Information: Current Affairs – A Single Special" on December 30, 1975. (That's one date I can never forget— probably because I still have the award notice framed and on my wall at home. Of all my things I did during Lisa's Wild Rides, that's the one that I keep closest to me.)

I will also never forget the Emmy Awards taping. My biggest concern was not would I win. It was who should I take with me and what will I wear? I anguished over my potential Emmy escort for months, but I really had no special man in my life at the time, so the "short list" of candidates was really short. I decided that, to be fair, I'd bring my writer and company partner, Charles. It certainly wasn't the most exciting date for that important night, but it did seem like the right thing to do. Deciding on my dress was easier. I passed on all of the flashy, glitzy gowns in my closet and picked a nightgown. Yep…a nightgown that I had bought for $20. It was black, long, and flowy with an empire waist, and it showed just enough cleavage to be interesting. When I put a large rhinestone brooch between my breasts, it was the perfect Emmy dress for me.

The taping started in the late afternoon then. We didn't have red carpet, live events in the '70s. The whole ceremony was a blur and still is. I'd been around movie and TV stars all my life, but this time, I was sitting with the best of the best! That was heady stuff. My concern wasn't about winning…I had already won just by getting the nomination! I only hoped that my family was watching. This was the most important achievement of my life! Good thing that I wasn't concerned about winning…because when they said, "And the award goes to…," they did not call out my name. But that really was okay with me.

By the time we were being driven back home in a long stretch limo, I had already found out that no one in my family was watching the Emmy show. Charles was dropped off first, and I rode alone to my apartment on Sweetzer Avenue, which I knew was empty. It was a beautiful, California night…with the kind of perfect weather that the Chamber of Commerce brags about. I sat on the stairs outside my apartment for a long time after the limo pulled away and watched the cars go by. Sometimes I'd hear some *Stairway to Heaven* or *Highway to Hell* blasting, and they both seemed real appropriate. That made me smile. A 20-something girl walked by. I didn't say hello and neither did she. I could tell that she was crying. I watched her until she was far down the sidewalk, out of my sight. Oh, baby…whatever's making you cry…I know where you are.

I stayed out there for a long time. I needed to think about what had just happened. I didn't think about not getting the Emmy. I thought about the other, more important "didn't happen" part of that evening. No one in my family was there—not in California sitting on the stairs with me, and not in their homes watching the show. Did Don Medford, hotshot director, ever sit in that elegant ceremony while they called his name as a nominee? No, he did not! But I was there. And who cared? Who really cared that Lisa Malouf Medford had been nominated for an Emmy award? No one cared. I sat outside my apartment a long time, but I could not hear the applause.

TEN

From the Back of the Limo to the Front

"Jovan! Get your hand off your dick, and get your ass in this limo!"

Jovan just stared at me for a few seconds before he broke out in a grin, went running over to the limo, and dove in head-first like he was going for a tackle! Yes, I was really talking that way to Jovan Belcher, the Kansas City Chiefs linebacker. I'd been driving him and his buddy, Samari Rolle (from the Ravens), around Vegas for two nights, and they needed to get with the program. They were great guys, but what part of, "Be outside when you told me you would be," didn't they get? I was trying to pick them up at The Hard Rock, and I'd been driving that 20-foot limo around and around the entry circle for too long, waiting for them to come out. First Samari showed, but when Jovan finally came out, what was going on? Jovan was standing there, smiling and talking to the crowd around him, holding a beer in one hand and doing a Michael Jackson—cupping his dick—with his other hand.

What the hell was I doing anyway? Jovan and Samari were my last ride of my last night of five years of working as a driver for Ambassador Limo. One of the other drivers asked me why I was retiring so soon. Soon? Take a good look, guy—a really good look. I'm 72 years old! That doesn't add up to "retiring so soon." Five years of lifting 600 pounds of luggage in and out of the trunk every night. Five years of telling barely-legal, way-too-drunk girls that they needed to stop trying to crawl out of the moon roof or it would be the last wedding shower (and anything else) they'd ever attend. How did I get to the front of the limo? Why wasn't I still riding around in the back?

Part of my journey to the black limo-driver's tuxedo and the aching back was the damn government's fault. Who the hell writes these fucking, no-good, money-grabbing tax laws? Not people who are busting their asses trying to build a business and employ people...and maybe eat well and buy just a few nice "trinkets" for themselves!

Not long after my Emmy night, I was producing a film for Dr. Terry Paulson on Assertive Management. My little company now had six employees instead of the original three, and we'd been doing great. At least I thought we were. This film was going to be Dr. Paulson's breakout venture into widespread education and public speaking. But it didn't happen the way we'd all planned. We made the film but ran out of money to distribute it. Well no, we didn't "run out of money"...the money was still there, but when I went to get it, I found out the tax guys thought they should get their nasty-ass hands on it! I think I should have checked my accountant's credentials a little better. Without any heads-up, he told me that all the money I had left—about $50,000—had to go for taxes! There was no money left to promote and distribute the film. Hell, there was barely enough to pay off my crew before I had to let them go! That took care of Visual Exchange, Inc.!

(It didn't set back Dr. Paulson too badly though. Today, he's an in-demand public speaker who gets like $10,000 for one speech. Interestingly, one of his most requested speeches is on Assertive Management, and his promo material uses the same words that I used in our film's brochure: "...finding the assertive middle ground between doormat and steamroller." You go, Terry!)

After Visual Exchange, I "wandered around" professionally for a few years. I still had enough money to live on for awhile—the IRS hadn't found every last penny—so I had a little time to think about what to be when I grew up—but certainly not forever!

I went to Vegas for awhile and dealt blackjack and tended bar. Nope, I didn't want to keep doing either of those jobs. The dealers' tips that had been so great in the '60s were going south in the '70s, and bartending was just too much "counseling" for my taste. Besides that irritation, the Mob didn't run Vegas anymore. I was much less excited about working in Vegas casinos without the "boys" around to watch over me.

Back to L.A. where, more for something to do than for any other reason, I took a job with Tools Plus working the phones to sell...you guessed it...tools. It was a nothing job, but one day, it brought my Vegas showgirl life crashing right into me again! When I'd be too bored to think straight, I'd lift up my blouse and flash the guys in the office. (That was what showgirls did.) One of the guys said, "You should meet this girl working in the back office. She does that flashing thing all the time too. I think she was a showgirl like you." I could see the Vegas lights and hear the applause again when I met Jeanie Stevenson at the Roach Coach for lunch that day. That was the first day of the next 30 years of being best friends.

Jeanie wasn't a showgirl in Vegas; she was one of those hard-working dancers. We started talking about the Vegas life and all the shows we were in. We were laughing about the really bad ones when I asked her to name the stupidest show she'd ever worked. She didn't remember the name or the lead performer, but she did remember that it had a beach ball in it. Oh my God! I was in that dumb show too! We had worked together in the George Gobel show, but we had never met. I was a showgirl, and she was a dancer. We had different dressing rooms and different people that we hung out with, so it wasn't strange that I'd never met her in Vegas. But it was strange to run into her at the Roach Coach in the parking lot of Tools Plus! We stood there for a minute and looked around together at the trash bins and the big air conditioner and the greasy back door into Tools Plus. This ain't Vegas, baby!

I found out that Jeanie (then Jeanie Stevens) was the girl in the story that everyone in Vegas knew and repeated for years! When Beldon Katleman owned the El Rancho, Jeanie was dancing there as the lead nude dancer. One night, Katleman went backstage and put his key down on her dressing table, and told her, "Come to my room tonight after the show."

When she replied with a quick, "No way," Katleman said, "If you don't, you won't have a job." (Like who wanted to sleep with him? Nobody!)

Jeanie went right to Barry Ashton, who was producing the show. Barry said, "Don't worry about it. You're not going to lose your job. It's that blond hair of yours. Just dye your hair." Suddenly, she was a redhead. Jeanie went on the next night and worked for four more months until it happened again! Katleman came in with the key...same conversation. The next day, Jeanie did another dye job, and then she had

jet-black hair! Katleman never bothered her again. (Guess
he only liked blondes or redheads.) That story had circulated
around the shows for two years, but I never knew who the girl
was. And there she was at Tools Plus! Vegas had just collided
with blue collar!

Jeanie Stevenson, lead dancer for every great show

Jeanie told me about working the Frontier when Howard Hughes owned it after 1967. She did an elaborate dance in the show that involved sliding down a ceiling-to-floor pole. After the number finished, the stage manager said, "You have a phone call." That was weird.

The man on the phone said, "This is Howard Hughes. I just want you to know how much I enjoyed your slide down the pole." She said she didn't believe that he was Hughes.

"Yes, this really is Howard Hughes. I'm your boss."

Her next question was, "How did you see me?" Jeanie was looking around to see if he was there. She didn't expect to find him though...no one had ever met Hughes, and he was never in the showroom.

"Oh, I can see everything; don't you worry." As he said that, Jeanie spotted the cameras that Hughes had installed all over the backstage. This was the late '60s. That kind of spy-shit just wasn't done...except by Howard Hughes.

I didn't stay at Tools Plus too long—it was pretty obvious that it wasn't a "career opportunity." I really did need to grow up. I needed to think about things I'd never heard talked about when I was a kid—retirement savings plans and pensions and health insurance. B-o-r-i-n-g shit! But there must be something to that crap. All of a sudden, all the friends my age were all about that stuff!

I wandered around a little more, taking some life side roads as a loan officer at a few Beverly Hills banks. (I gave up flashing in the banking business.) I also tried my hand as an accountant for Disney and Warner Brothers and as a production accountant for several "Movies of the Week." I settled in at Sony Studios and completed my time there as the Prop and Warehouse Manager. I was a "regular" employee... for 14 years! That's the longest time that I had ever done anything in my entire life—which included holding down jobs, staying with marriages or boyfriends, living in one apartment, and keeping the same major appliances. Of course, none of those other things had pensions and super-cheap, life-time medical insurance! I had done it. I had become an adult. I couldn't hear much applause, that's for sure, but today, the crinkle of the envelope when I pull out my pension check is also music to my ears.

Finally escaping from Sony, I returned to the place where the applause had been the loudest—Las Vegas. So there I was, hollering at my football player customers to get in the damn limo and roaring off into the night—all of us laughing our asses off!

Epilogue

It's been over 50 years since my first history-making opening in Vegas, which started Lisa's Wild Ride. Today, I am just where I want to be. I have a lovely, comfortable home in an age-restricted community high in the hills south of Vegas. It's beautiful up here and quiet. If two cars come down my road in an hour, I think it's a parade. It's the way it's supposed to be.

The best part is that from one spot in my back yard, I can look down and see the lights of the Vegas Strip shimmering like a sea of jewels below…and I remember.

I can still hear the applause.

"Making Book"

Author Bios

Jeanne Gulbranson and her husband Bill were doing the daily walk-the-dog-around-the-block when, for the first time, their new neighbor appeared in her front yard. She was holding a solar light and looked perplexed. But it wasn't the light that attracted Jeanne's attention. "Oh my God," Jeanne said. "Look at those legs! I thought this neighborhood was age-restricted. How did those legs get in here?"

Bill either knew better than to comment, or maybe he wasn't able to speak. Whatever...

They had both seen her license plate in the driveway that read, "1STNUDE", and had wondered if they were interpreting that correctly. First Nude. Who would drive around with that on their car?

"Bill," Jeanne insisted, "go over there and see if she needs some help with that light. And find out what that license plate means." Bill hesitated appropriately to make sure that he was really being directed to talk to the woman with The Legs. "Yes, do it Bill...just go over there," Jeanne repeated.

Jeanne was curious, and she was not stupid. She stayed on the sidewalk to keep an eye on the discussion and on the discussers.

A few minutes later, the light was again working and Bill returned with his report. "Yep, it really means First Nude—because she was the first nude showgirl in Vegas. Her name's Lisa Medford." Simply amazing.

That was the beginning of Lisa and Jeanne's partnering to write *I Can Hear the Applause.* From the start, it was an improbable pairing of authors. Lisa had been a showgirl and an actress. She still wore 4" heels and had a cell phone permanently affixed to her ear. Jeanne was a consultant specializing in business strategy with a real affinity for sensible pumps and PowerPoint presentations in boardrooms. It was like putting together a flamingo and a penguin. But it worked.

Lisa Malouf Medford's biography—what can be included here that you haven't just already read? Lisa told the stories and Jeanne Gulbranson put together the words to build out the life-tales that married up into chapters to present Lisa Medford's many lives. The result was *I Can Hear the Applause: Adult Language...Some Nudity.*

In addition to too many corporate white papers and articles, Jeanne has authored two previously published books: *Be the Horse or the Jockey: 110 Tips and Techniques for Followers... and Leaders* and *Pink Leadership: 15 Life Lessons for ♀ Leaders.* Each of the books received the Finalist Award from the 2009 Next Generation Indie Book Awards. Additional information about her previously published works can be found on Jeanne's literary site (www.jeannegulbranson.com).

These are the women who either lived (or wrote about) Lisa's Wild Ride.

Index

Made in the USA
Lexington, KY
10 December 2012